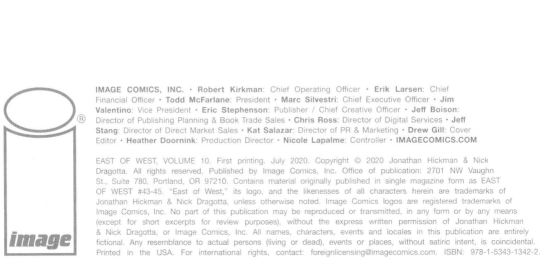

IMAGE COMICS, INC. • **Robert Kirkman**: Chief Operating Officer • **Erik Larsen**: Chief Financial Officer • **Todd McFarlane**: President • **Marc Silvestri**: Chief Executive Officer • **Jim Valentino**: Vice President • **Eric Stephenson**: Publisher / Chief Creative Officer • **Jeff Boison**: Director of Publishing Planning & Book Trade Sales • **Chris Ross**: Director of Digital Services • **Jeff Stang**: Director of Direct Market Sales • **Kat Salazar**: Director of PR & Marketing • **Drew Gill**: Cover Editor • **Heather Doornink**: Production Director • **Nicole Lapalme**: Controller • **IMAGECOMICS.COM**

EAST OF WEST

JONATHAN HICKMAN
WRITER

NICK DRAGOTTA
ARTIST

FRANK MARTIN
COLORS

RUS WOOTON
LETTERS

EAS
W

T

OF

EST

WE'VE TAKEN EVERYTHING
YOU **LOVE.**

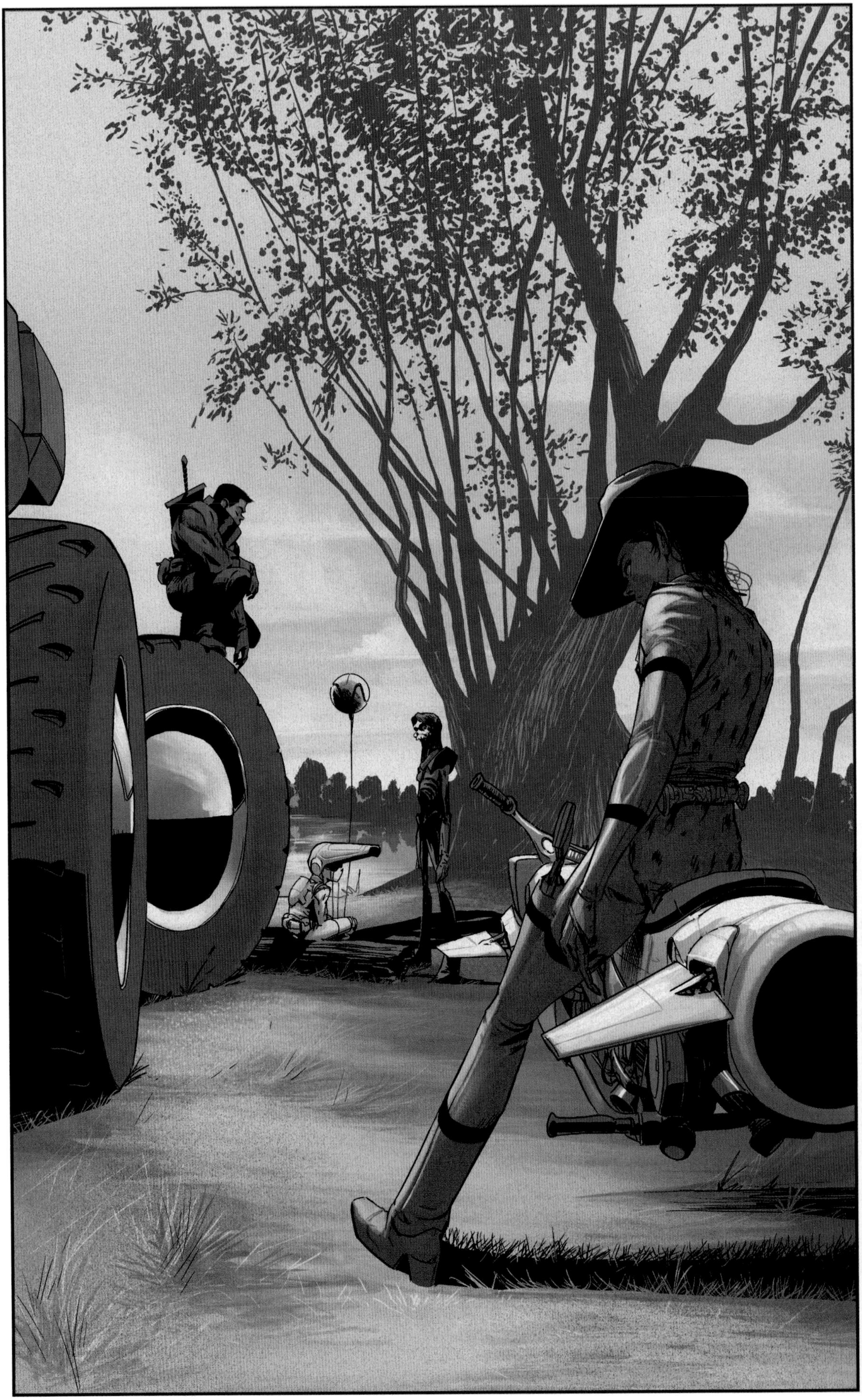

Well... Did you **hurt him?** Or did you do what you promised and **let my dad be?**

We made a deal *you and I*...and I won't be the one to break it.

Your father though -- *being how he is and who he is* -- is the man you need to worry about. That one doesn't let things go, especially things like you, so I would expect him -- and sooner rather than later.

Yeah, but how's he going to know where to find us?

Oh. I told him.

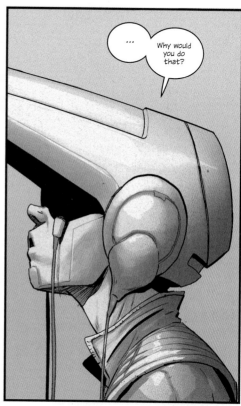

... Why would you do that?

Old business between War and Death...

No point digging any deeper than that... at least not until you're capable of understanding this world of man...

And how it shapes the *nature* of all who live in it.

So... you ready to go to school?

It's a *short walk* to begin the *long journey* of becoming the **Great Beast.**

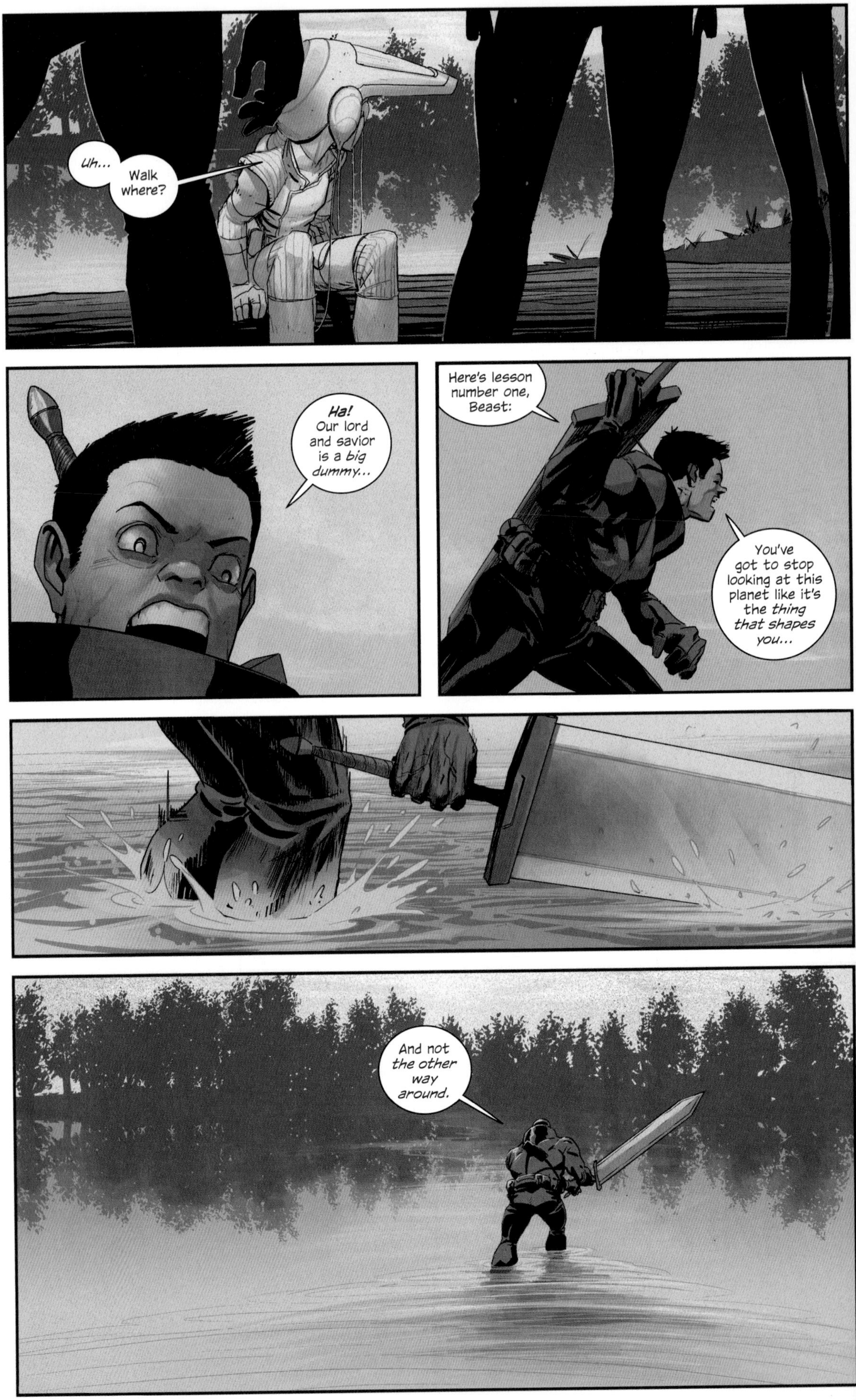

Uh...
Walk where?
Ha! Our lord and savior is a *big dummy...*
Here's lesson number one, Beast:
You've got to stop looking at this planet like it's the *thing that shapes* you...
And not *the other* way *around.*

See *truth*, Babylon...

There's no obstacle that cannot be *destroyed* -- nothing standing between you and where you want to go that cannot be *cleaved asunder.*

When two or more of us are *gathered together*...we can move more freely than man in man's *own* world.

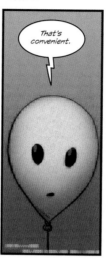

That's convenient.

RRAARRRR!

THOOM!

So we travel in ways that your father cannot.

And if he wants to find us...

He will have to find some other way there.

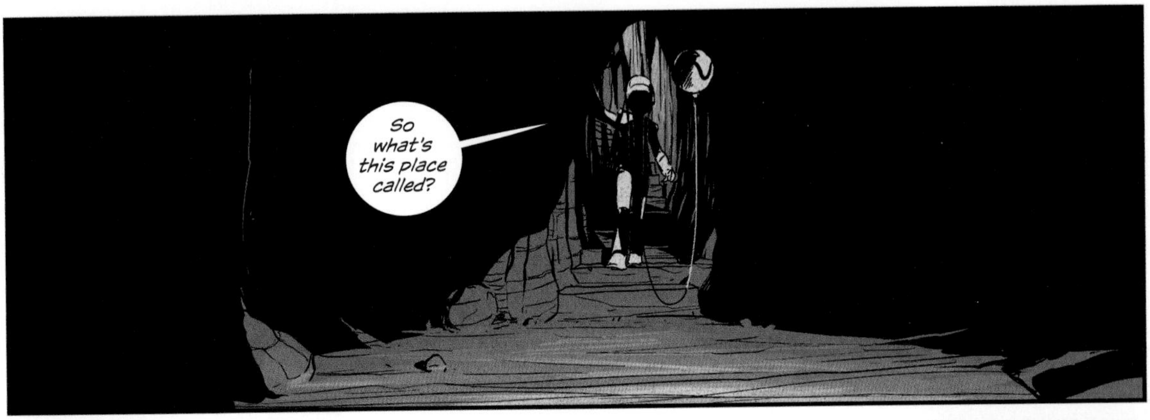
So what's this place called?

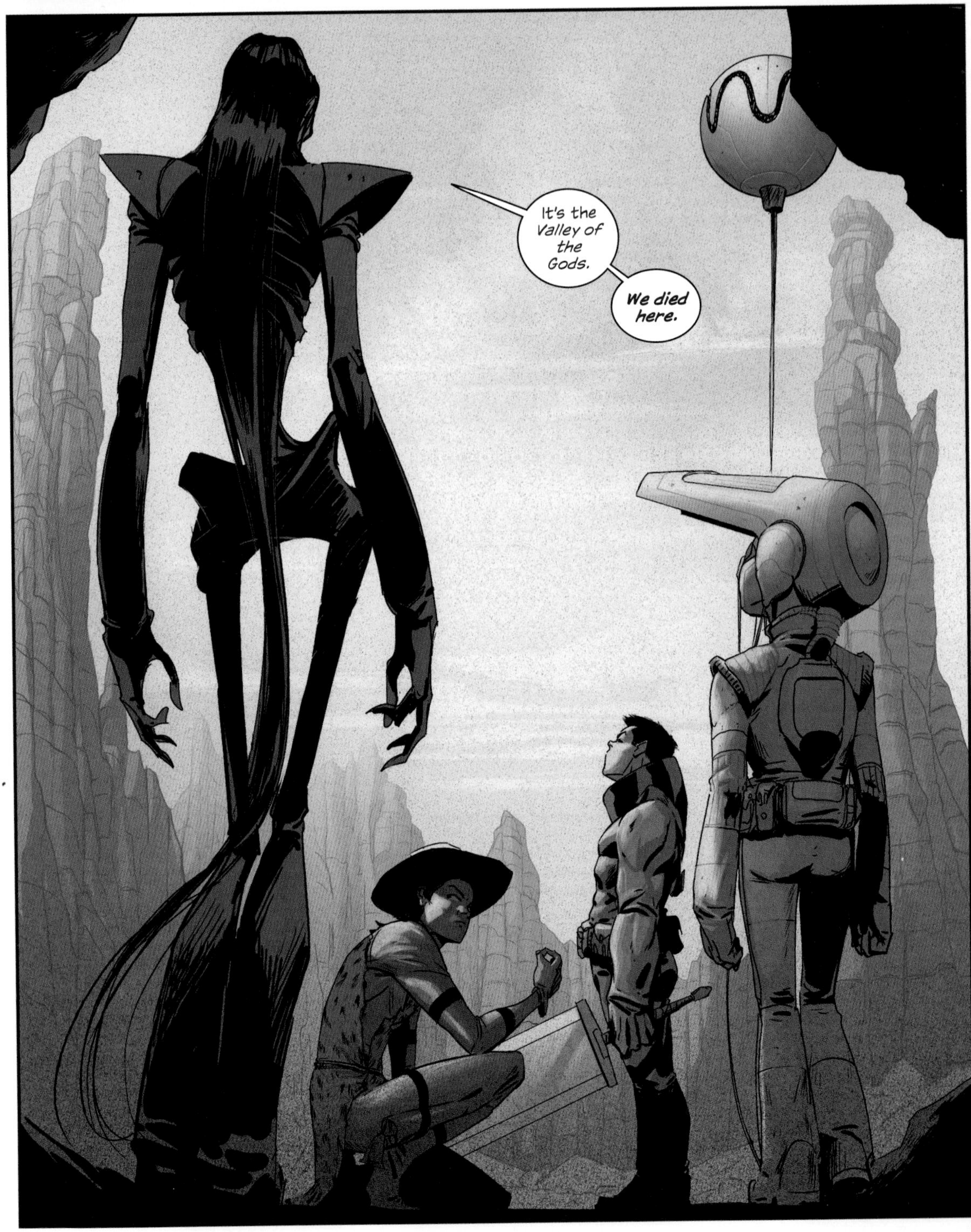
It's the Valley of the Gods.
We died here.

LET'S SEE IF YOU CAN
TAKE IT BACK.

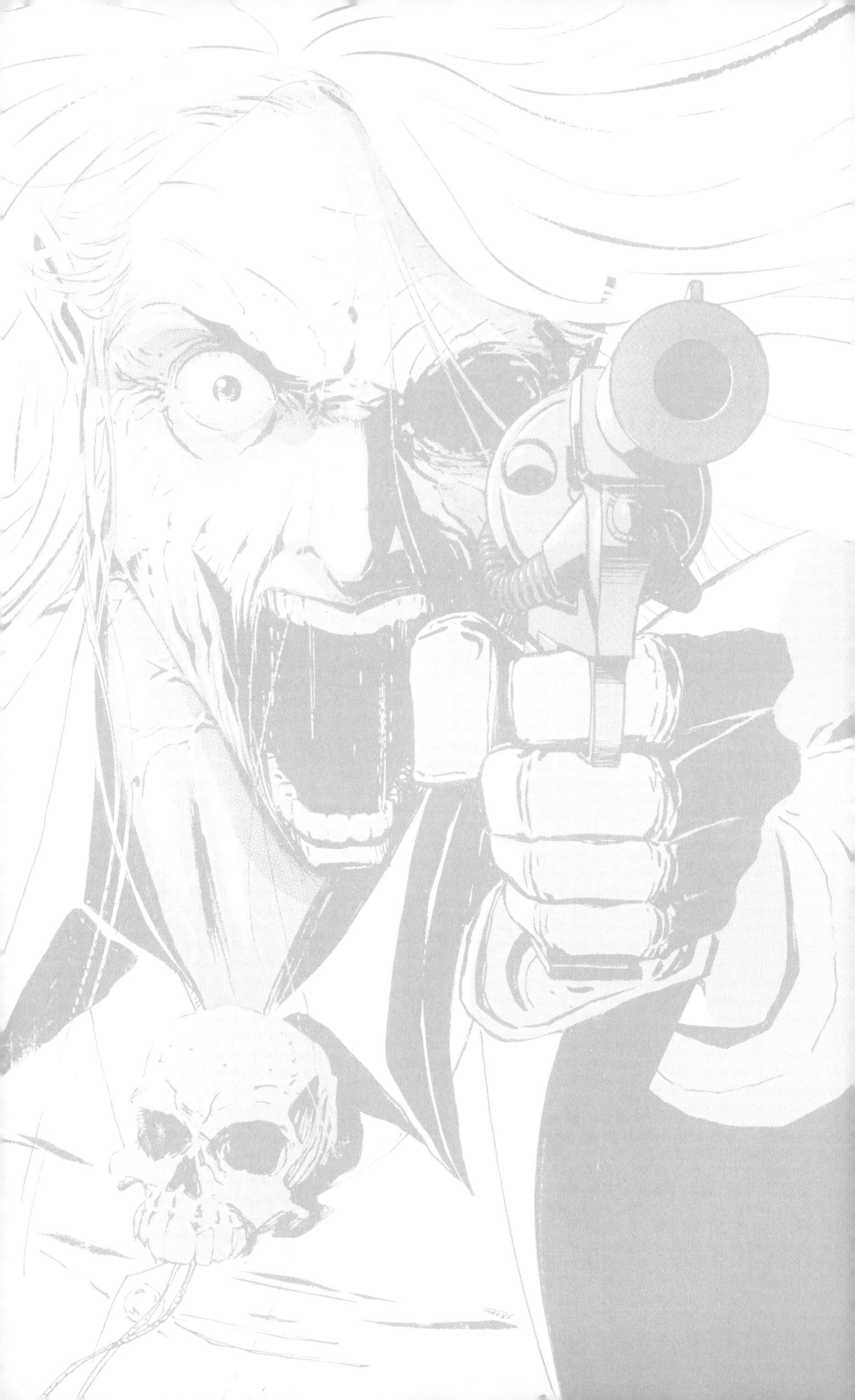

43

FORTY-THREE:
THIS IS **WAR**

Near Armistice.

This is the worst part...

The waiting.

Don't be foolish, John. This is nowhere near the worst of it.

Soon, out there on some godforsaken stretch of land, people will be **dying** for their **flag**...

Taking orders from leaders who say they care for their people, but act as if they don't...

In a conflict that's become a conflict because they just *can't help themselves...* and cannot *control their nature.*

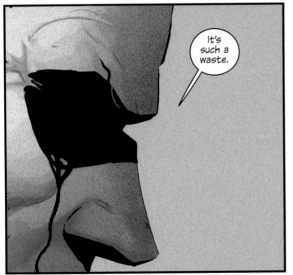

It's such a waste.

Why are you talking like our hands are clean in all this, Wolf?

Brother... **they are not.**

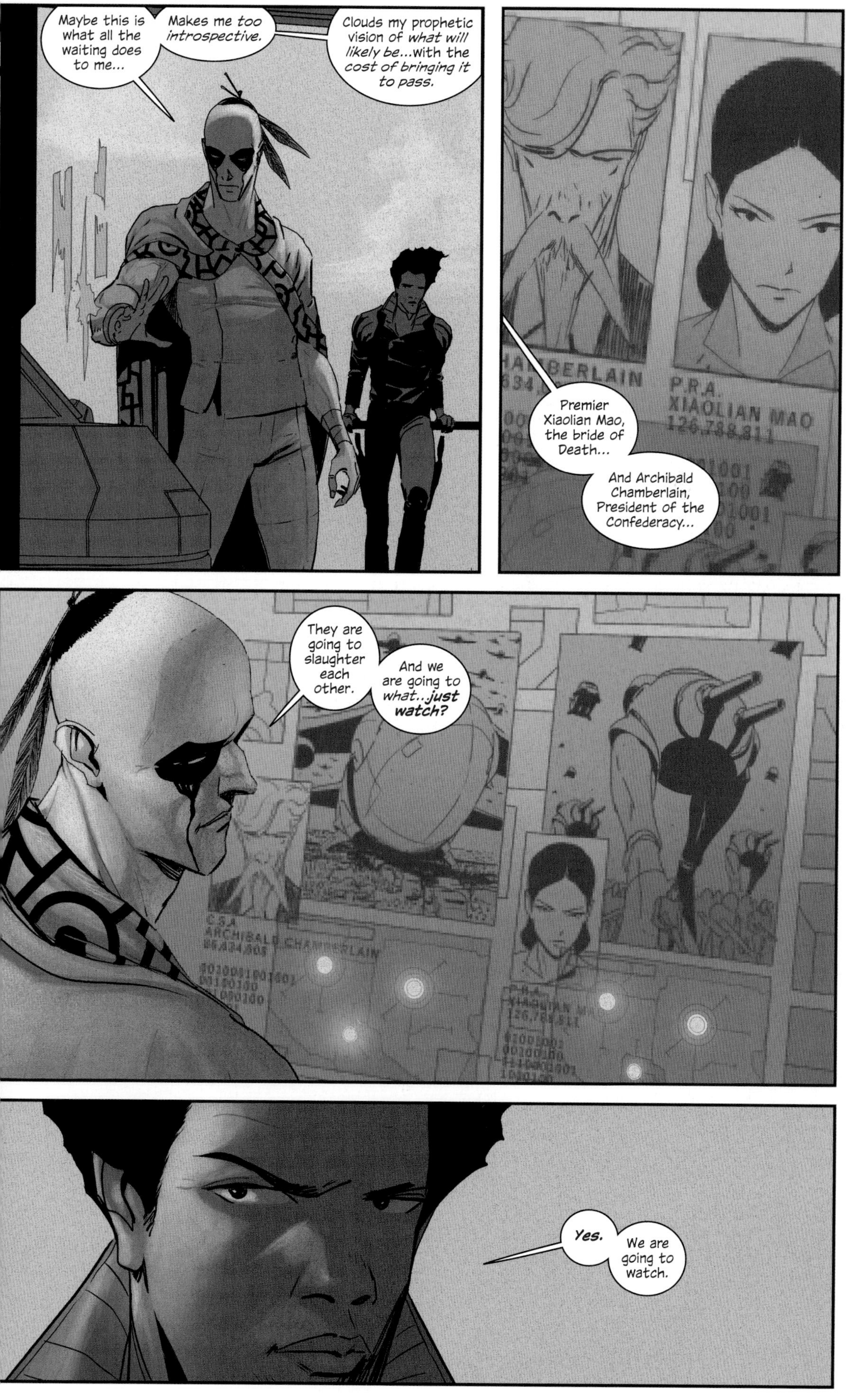
Maybe this is what all the waiting does to me...
Makes me *too introspective.*
Clouds my prophetic vision of *what will likely be*...with the *cost of bringing it to pass.*
P.R.A.
XIAOLIAN MAO
Premier Xiaolian Mao, the bride of Death...
And Archibald Chamberlain, President of the Confederacy...
They are going to slaughter each other.
And we are going to *what...**just watch?***
Yes.
We are going to watch.

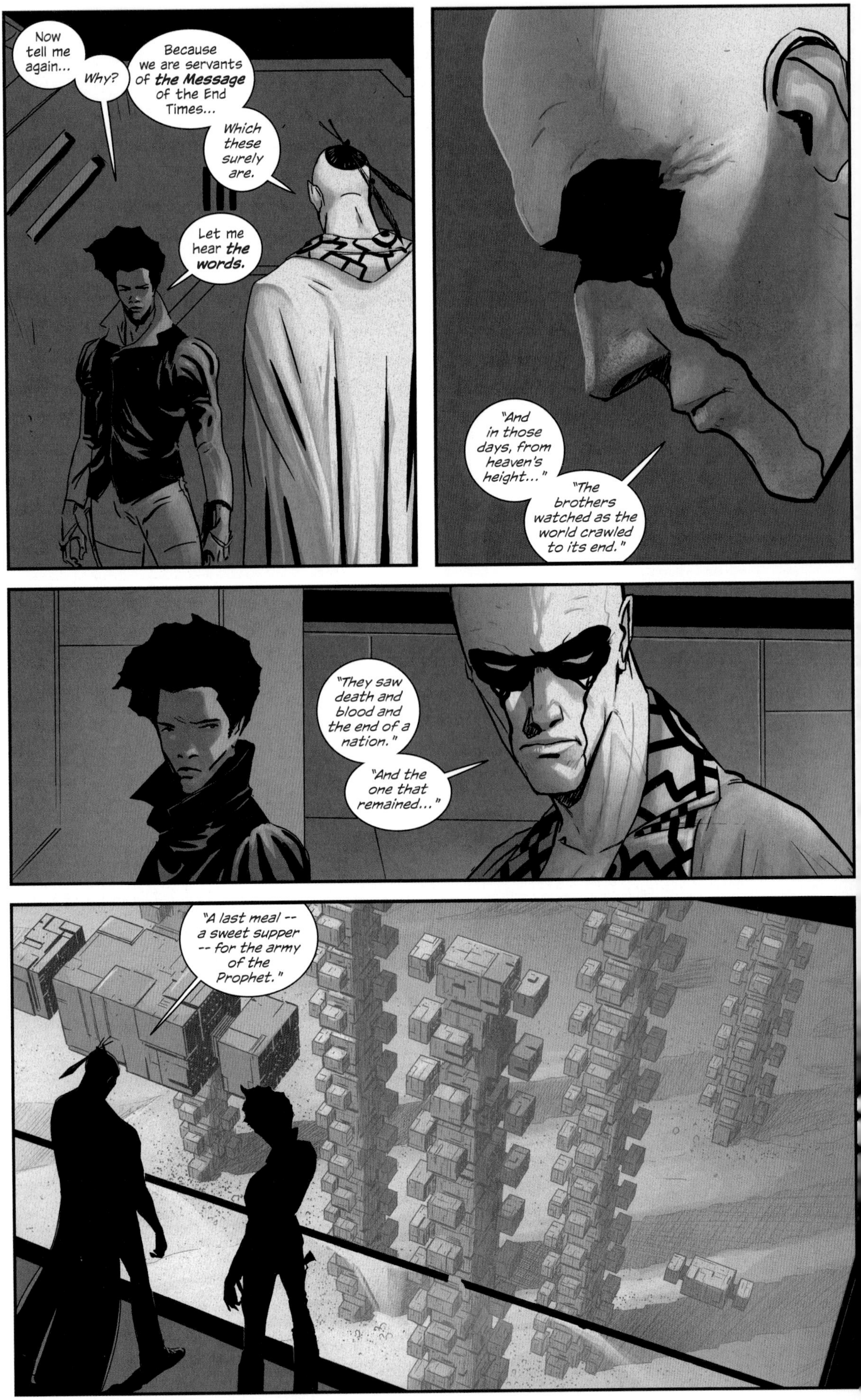
Now tell me again...
Why?
Because we are servants of ***the Message*** of the End Times...
Which these surely are.
Let me hear **the words.**
"And in those days, from heaven's height..."
"The brothers watched as the world crawled to its end."
"They saw death and blood and the end of a nation."
"And the one that remained..."
"A last meal -- a sweet supper -- for the army of the Prophet."

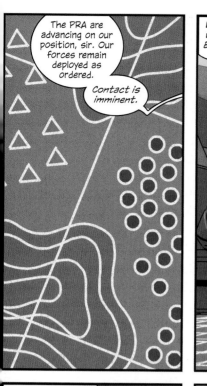

The PRA are advancing on our position, sir. Our forces remain deployed as ordered.

Contact is imminent.

Well, well, Bel...

It seems that our ill intent and infernal machinations have finally delivered unto us the closure that we so dearly seek.

Are you as *thrilled* as I am at the prospect of **victory**?

Go to hell.

No? Fear not, old friend, for I am downright inflamed and my full measure is enough for the both of us.

Sir! We have contact! And there appear to be more forces than we expected!

Thousands more!

Thank you, General...

Hrmpt!

Total commitment from our enemies...

Do you like these stakes, Mister Solomon? All in, as it were, for the rabble?

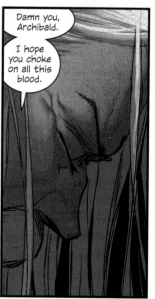

Damn you, Archibald.

I hope you choke on all this blood.

"Choke? No, dear Bel..."

"I will drink it all."

"General...tell our forces to **hold**."

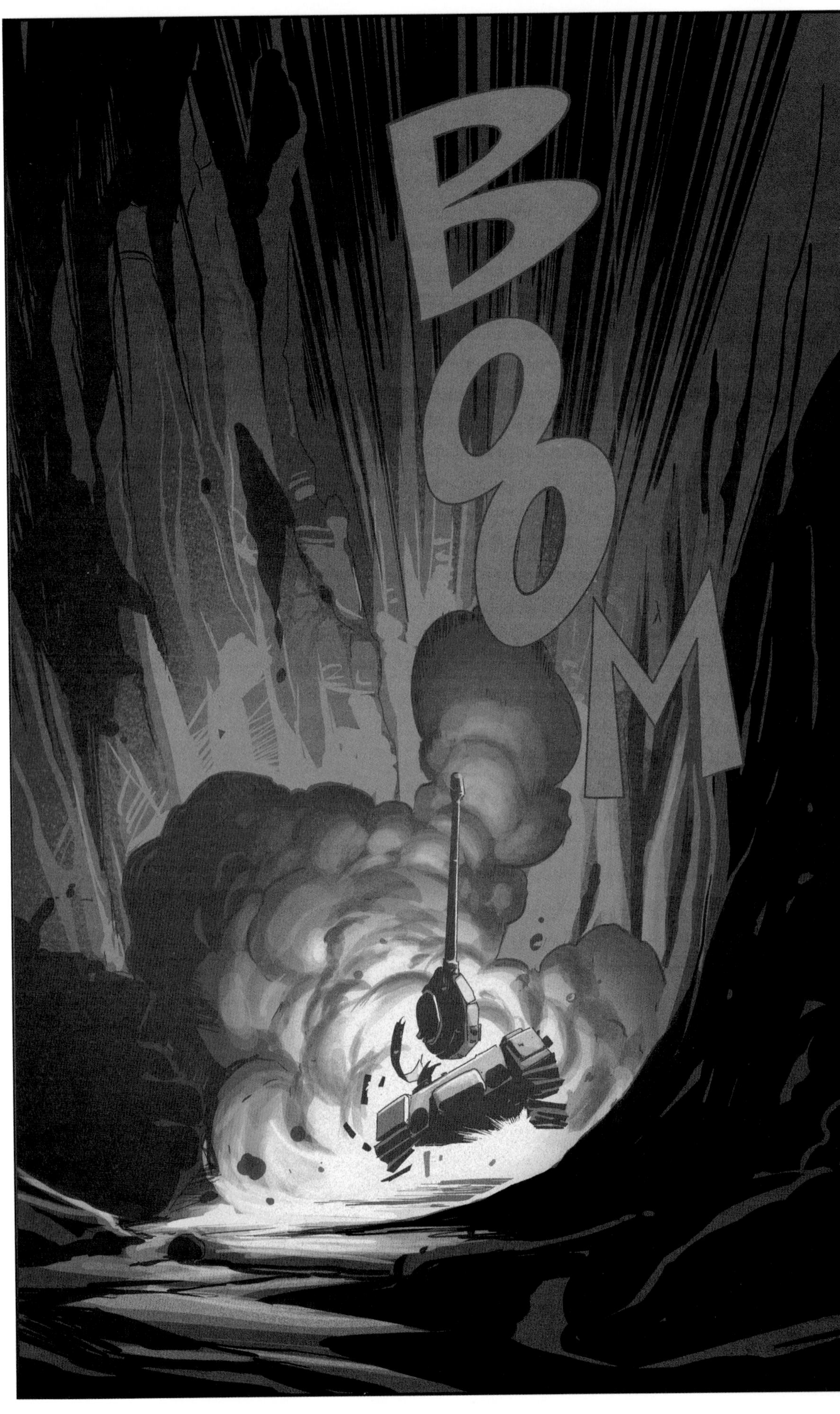
BOOM

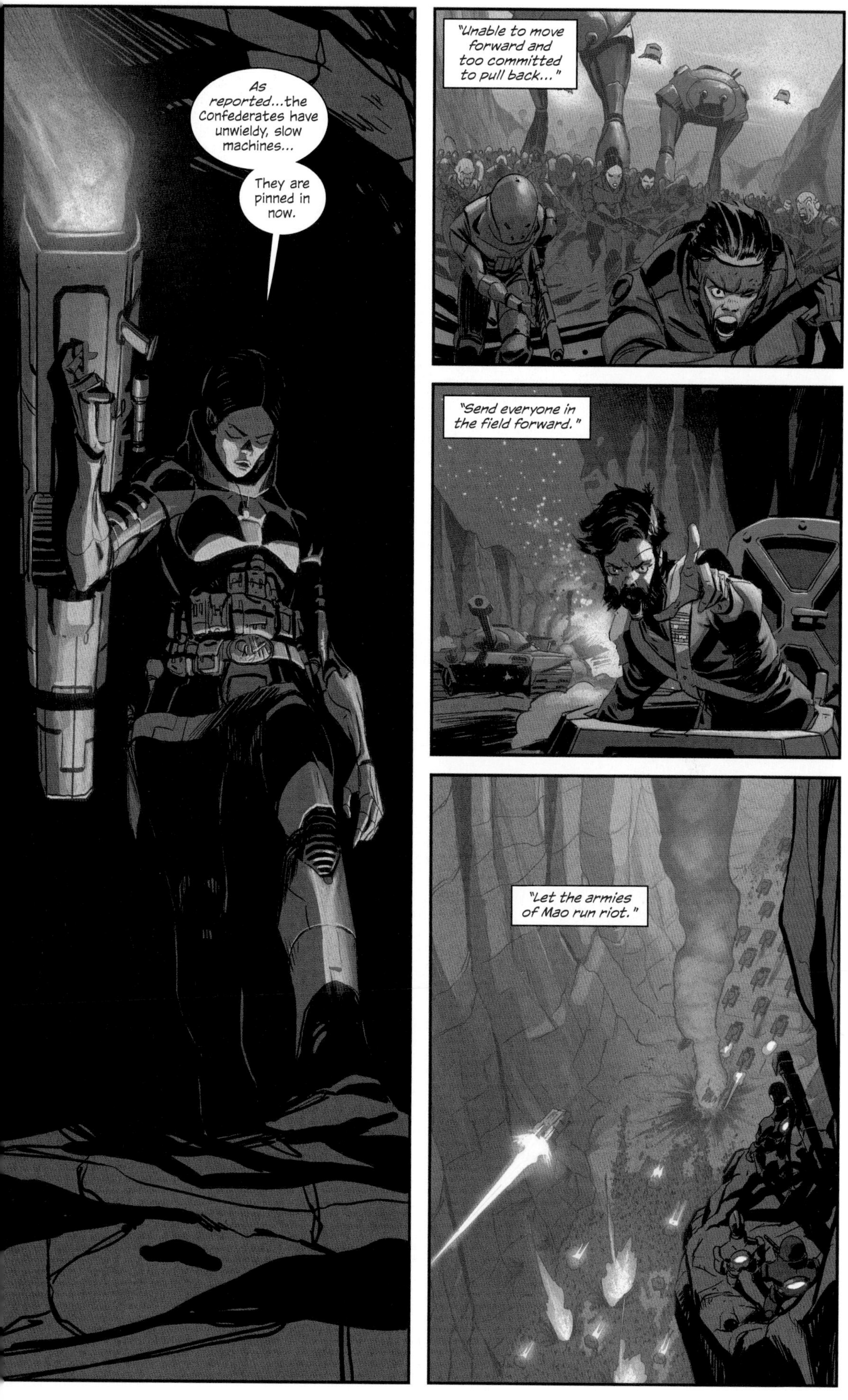
As reported...the Confederates have unwieldy, slow machines...
They are pinned in now.
"Unable to move forward and too committed to pull back..."
"Send everyone in the field forward."
"Let the armies of Mao run riot."

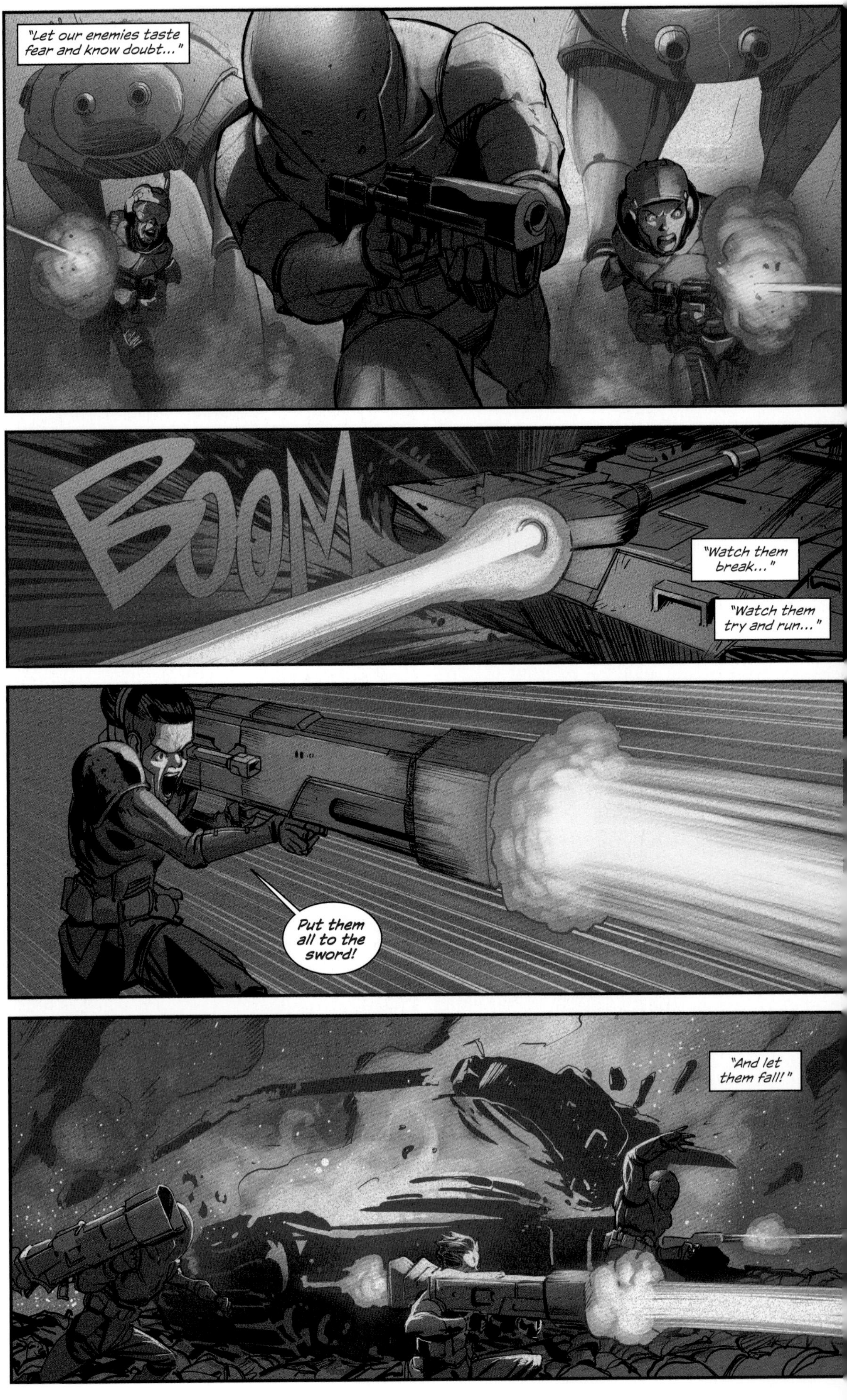
"Let our enemies taste fear and know doubt..."
BOOM
"Watch them break..."
"Watch them try and run..."
Put them all to the sword!
"And let them fall!"

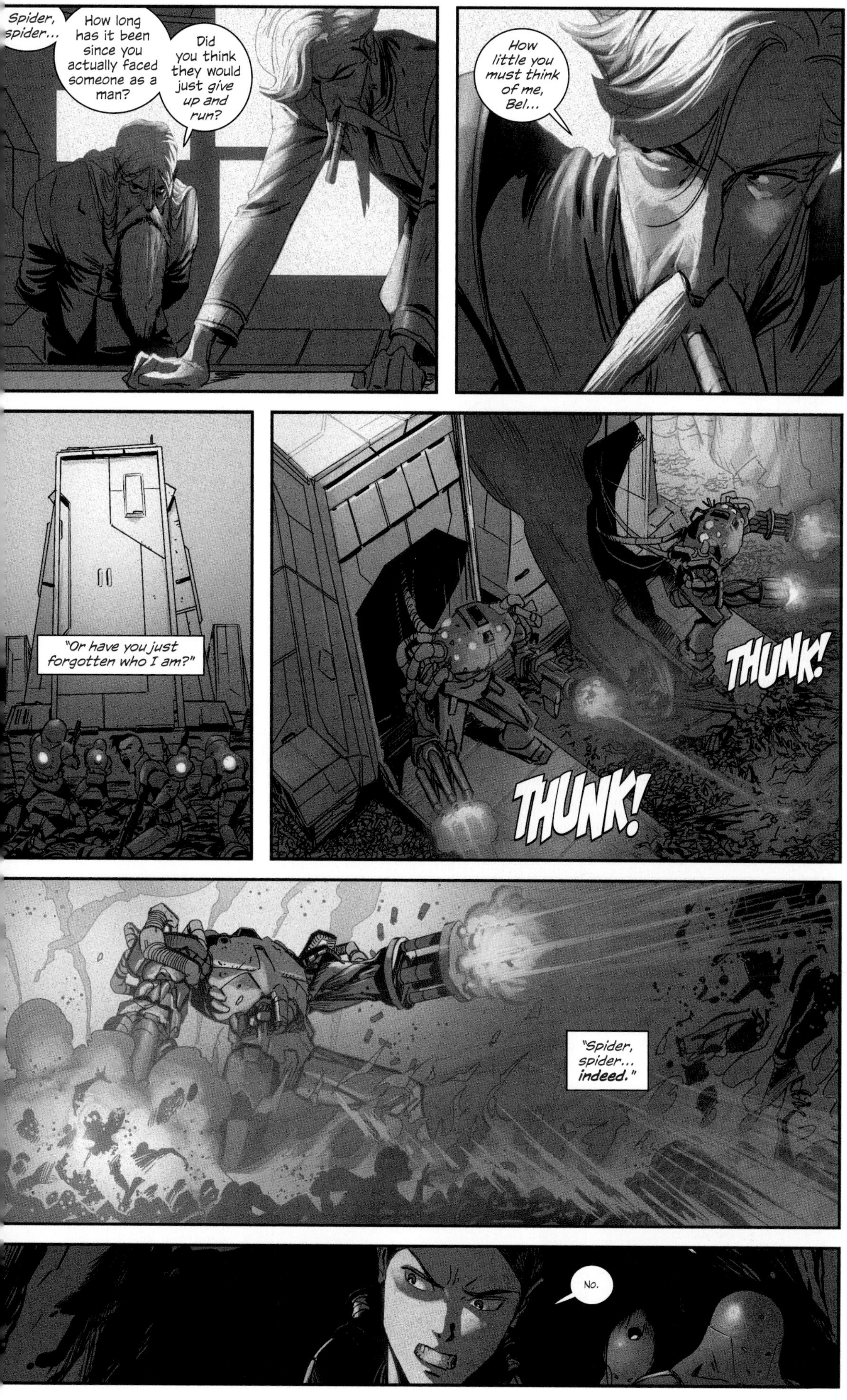
Spider, spider...
How long has it been since you actually faced someone as a man?
Did you think they would just give up and run?
How little you must think of me, Bel...
"Or have you just forgotten who I am?"
THUNK!
THUNK!
"Spider, spider... indeed."
No.

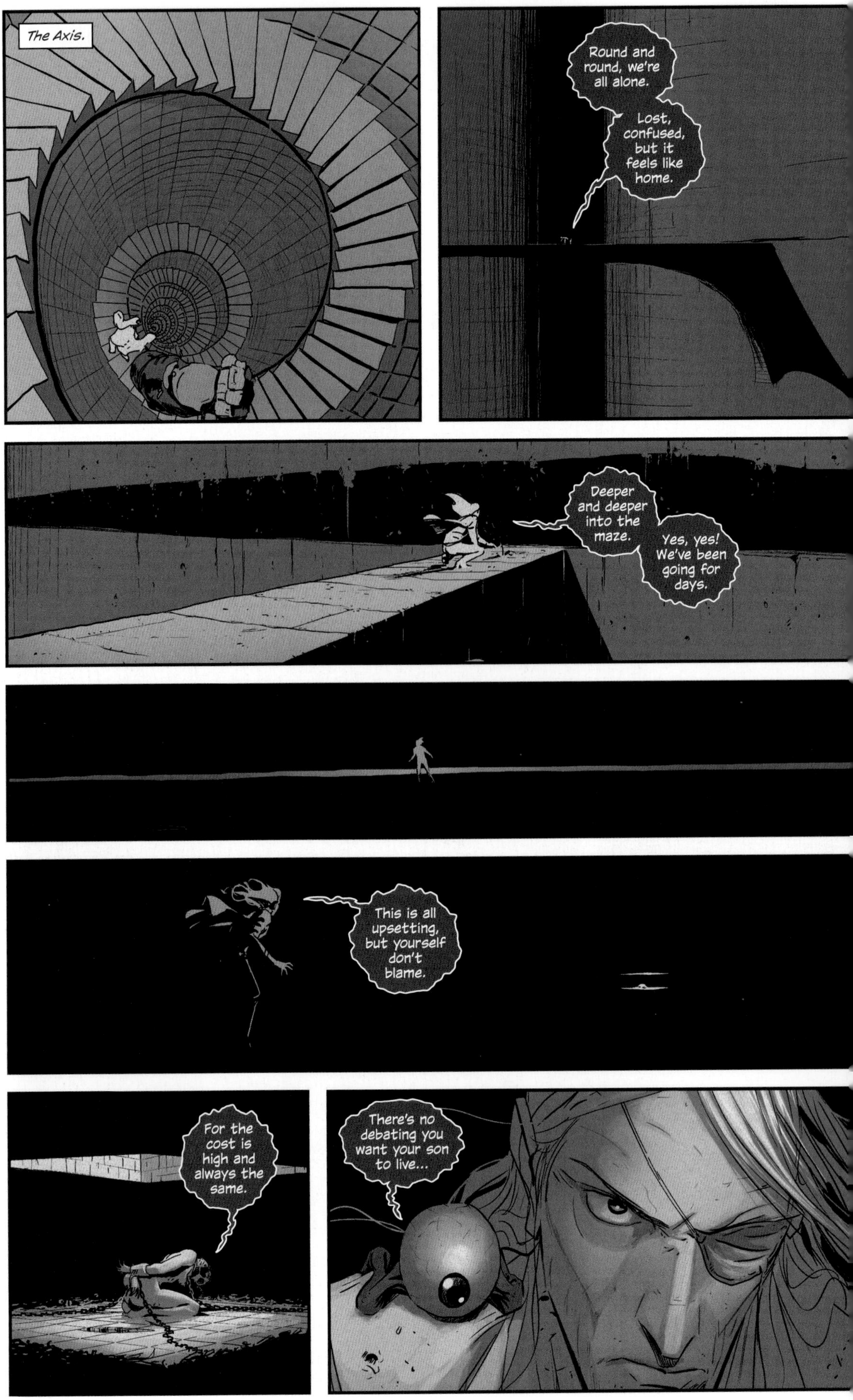
The Axis.
Round and round, we're all alone.
Lost, confused, but it feels like home.
Deeper and deeper into the maze.
Yes, yes! We've been going for days.
This is all upsetting, but yourself don't blame.
For the cost is high and always the same.
There's no debating you want your son to live...

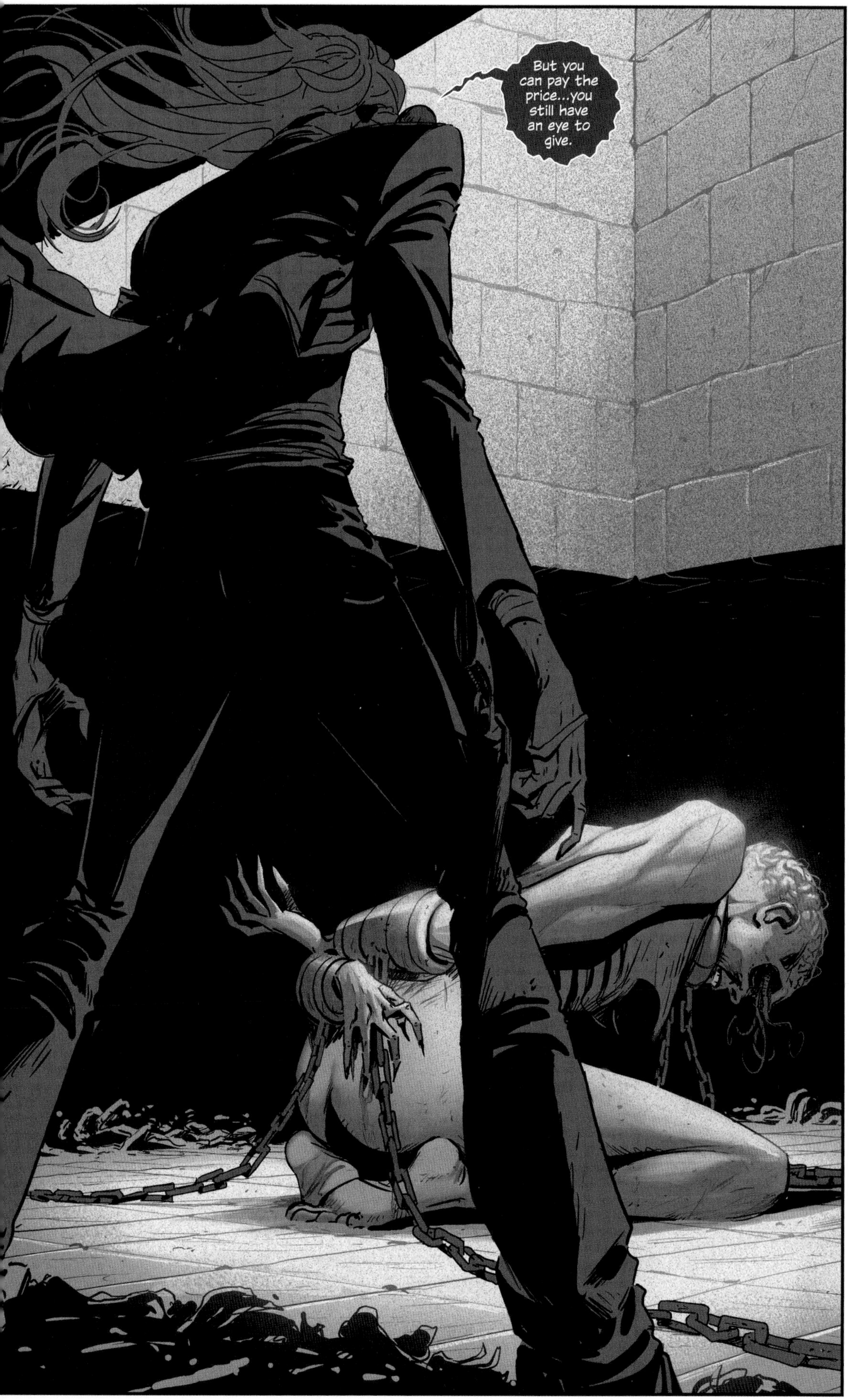
But you can pay the price...you still have an eye to give.

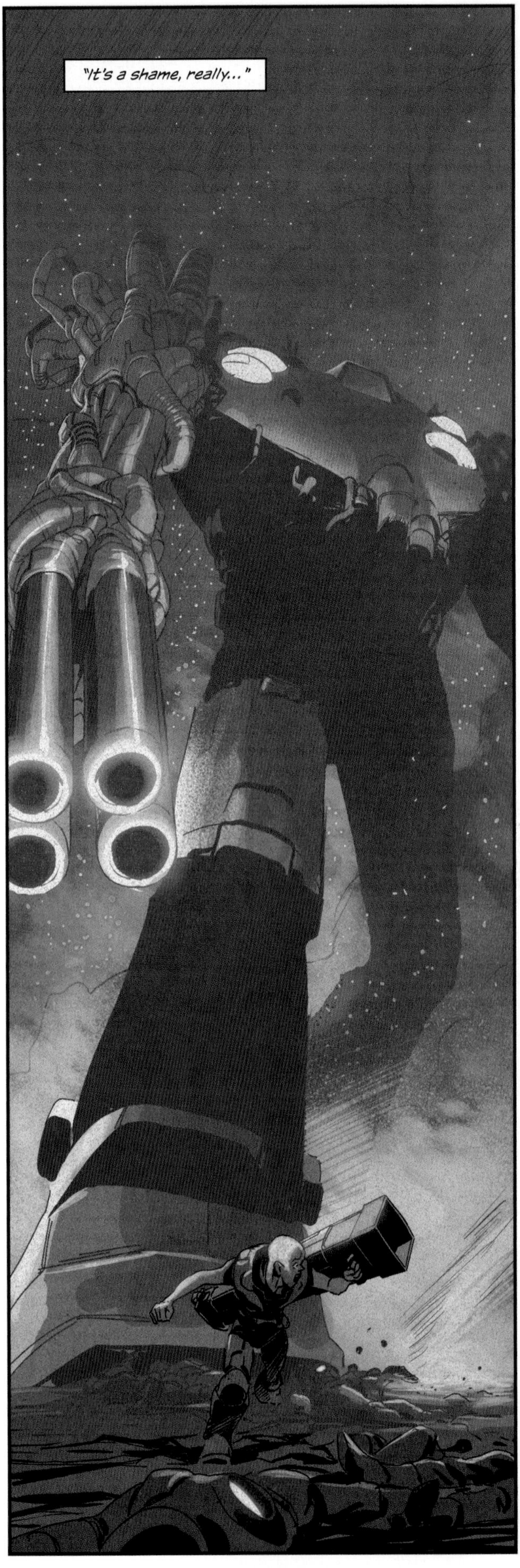
"It's a shame, really..."

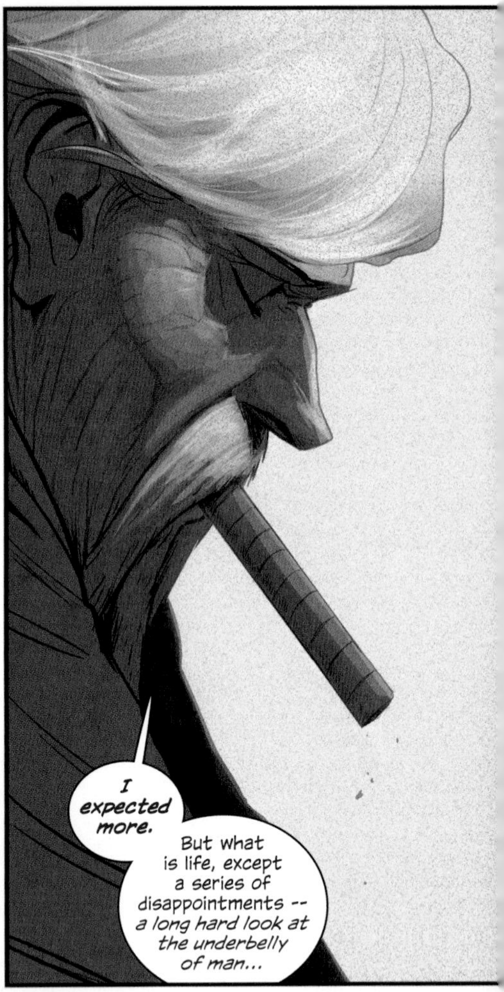
I expected more.
But what is life, except a series of disappointments -- a long hard look at the underbelly of man...

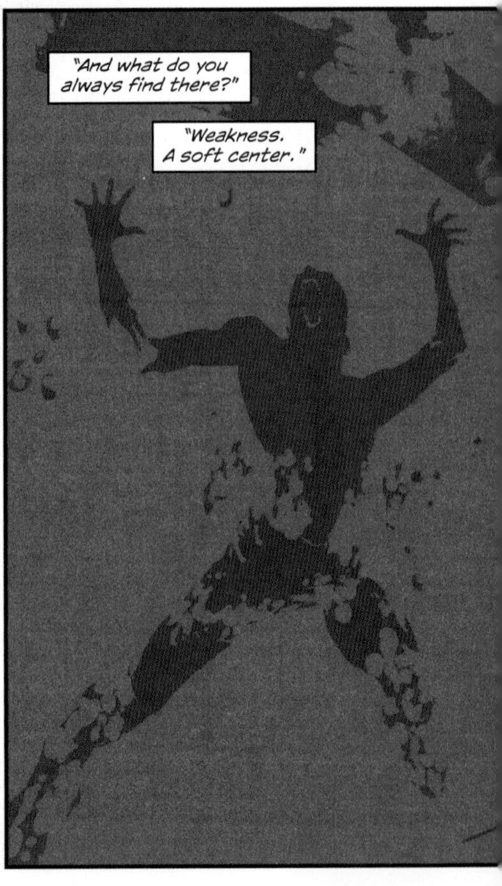
"And what do you always find there?"
"Weakness. A soft center."

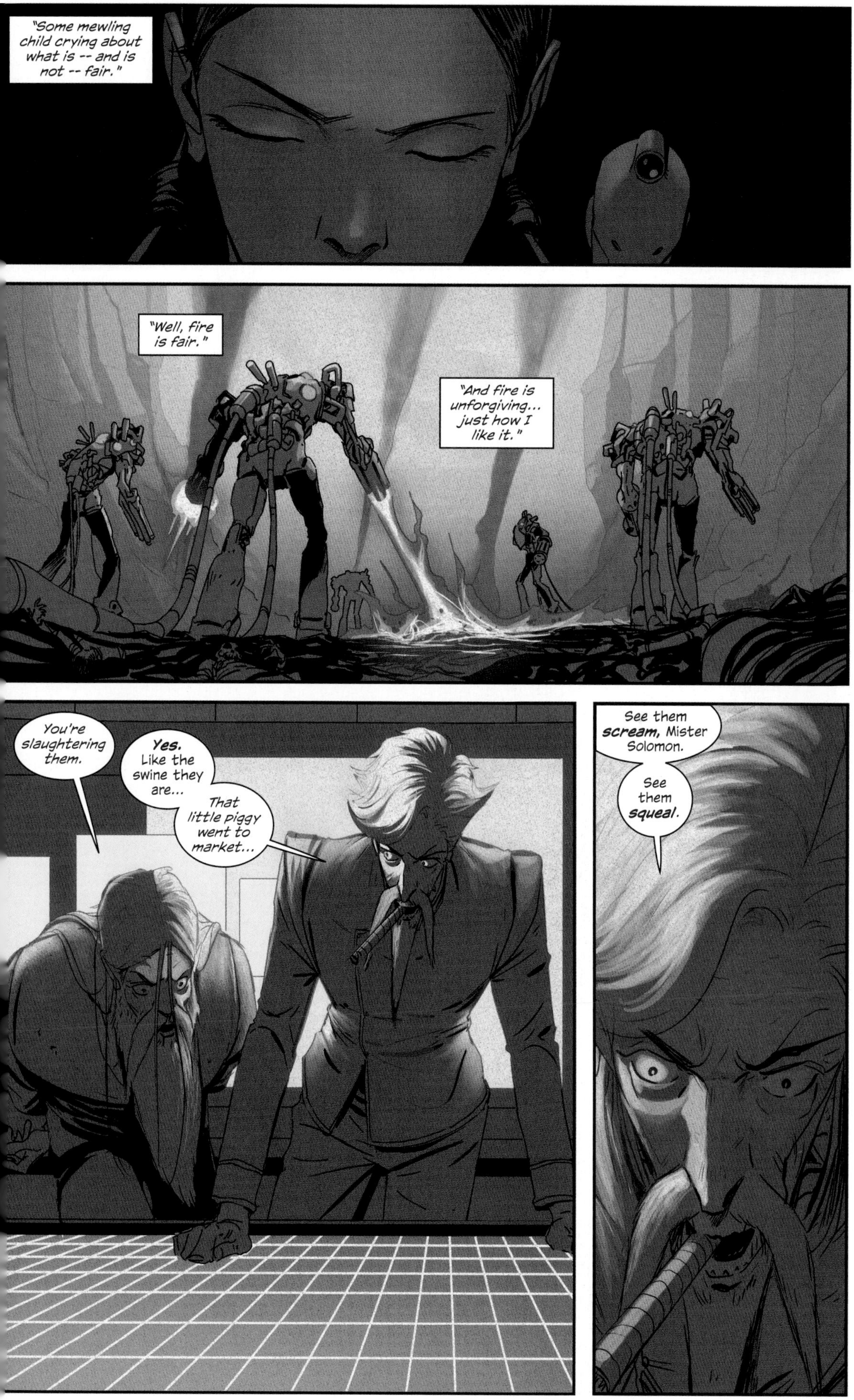
"Some mewling child crying about what is -- and is not -- fair."
"Well, fire is fair."
"And fire is unforgiving... just how I like it."
You're slaughtering them.
Yes. Like the swine they are...
That little piggy went to market...
See them scream, Mister Solomon.
See them squeal.

"We're not just ending a nation here today...we are putting an end to a rival for all time."

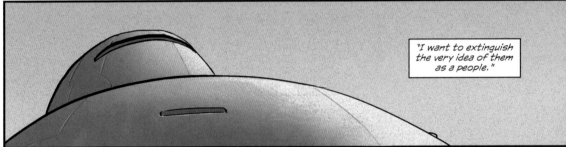

"I want to extinguish the very idea of them as a people."

"I want them erased from history..."

Do you know what that is called, Bel?

What, goddamn you? What?

It is called...

VICTORY!

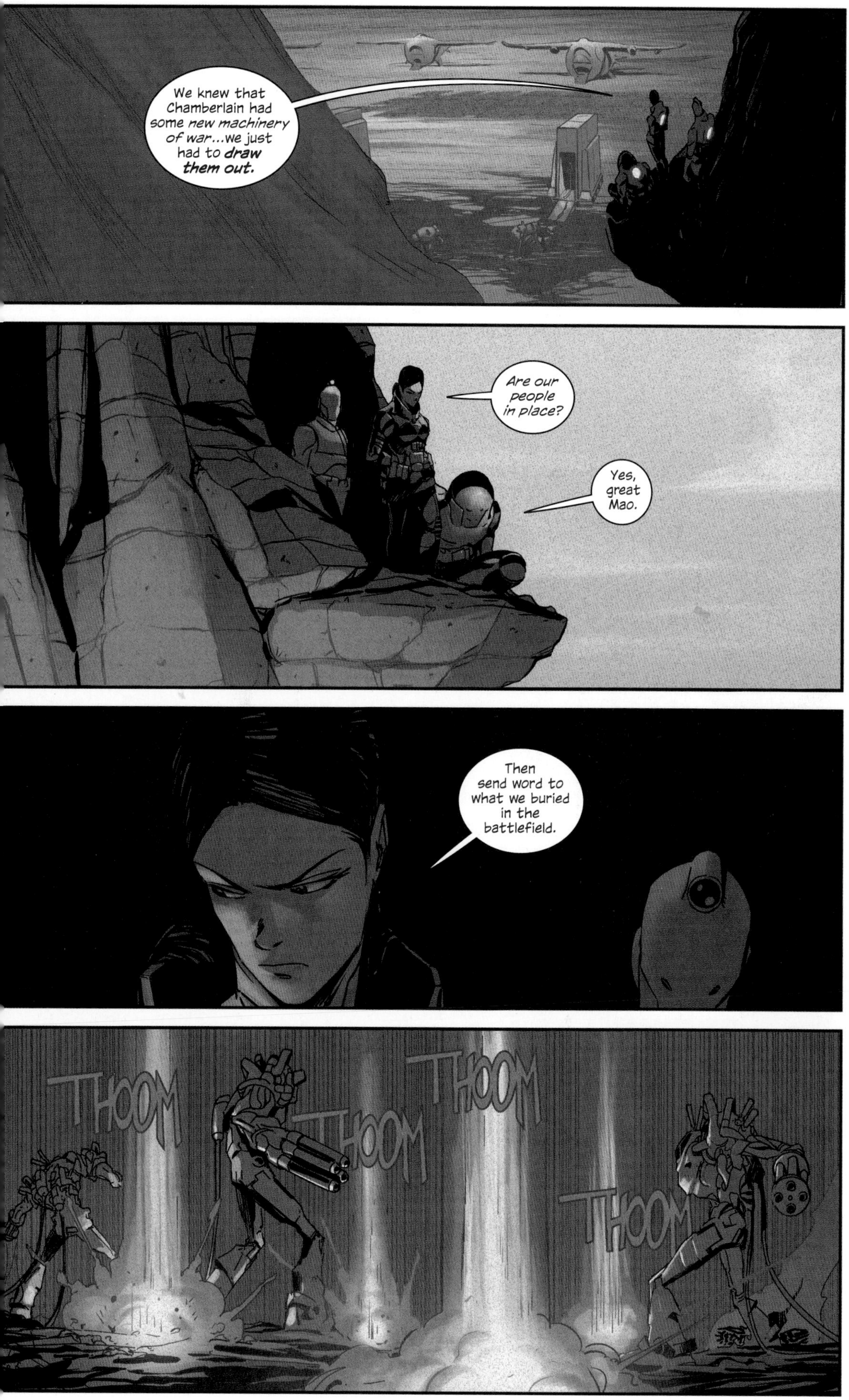

We knew that Chamberlain had some *new machinery of war*...we just had to ***draw them out.***
Are our people in place?
Yes, great Mao.
Then send word to what we buried in the battlefield.
THOOM
THOOM
THOOM
THOOM

"We have a gift for you Confederates..."

"I've sent Dragons."

"I've sent Widowmakers."

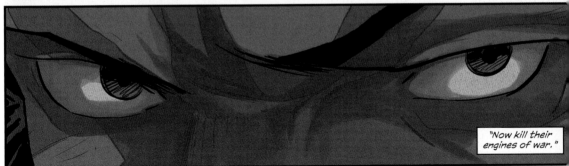

"Now kill their engines of war."

I have a *gift* for you, soldier...

From a *real warrior* and not a *child with a gun*...

KRASH!

Greetings from Mao.

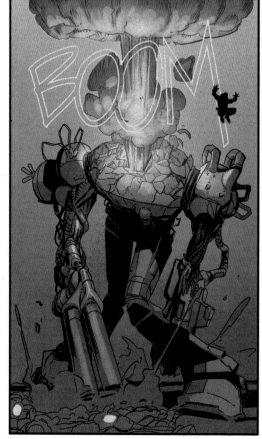

BOOM

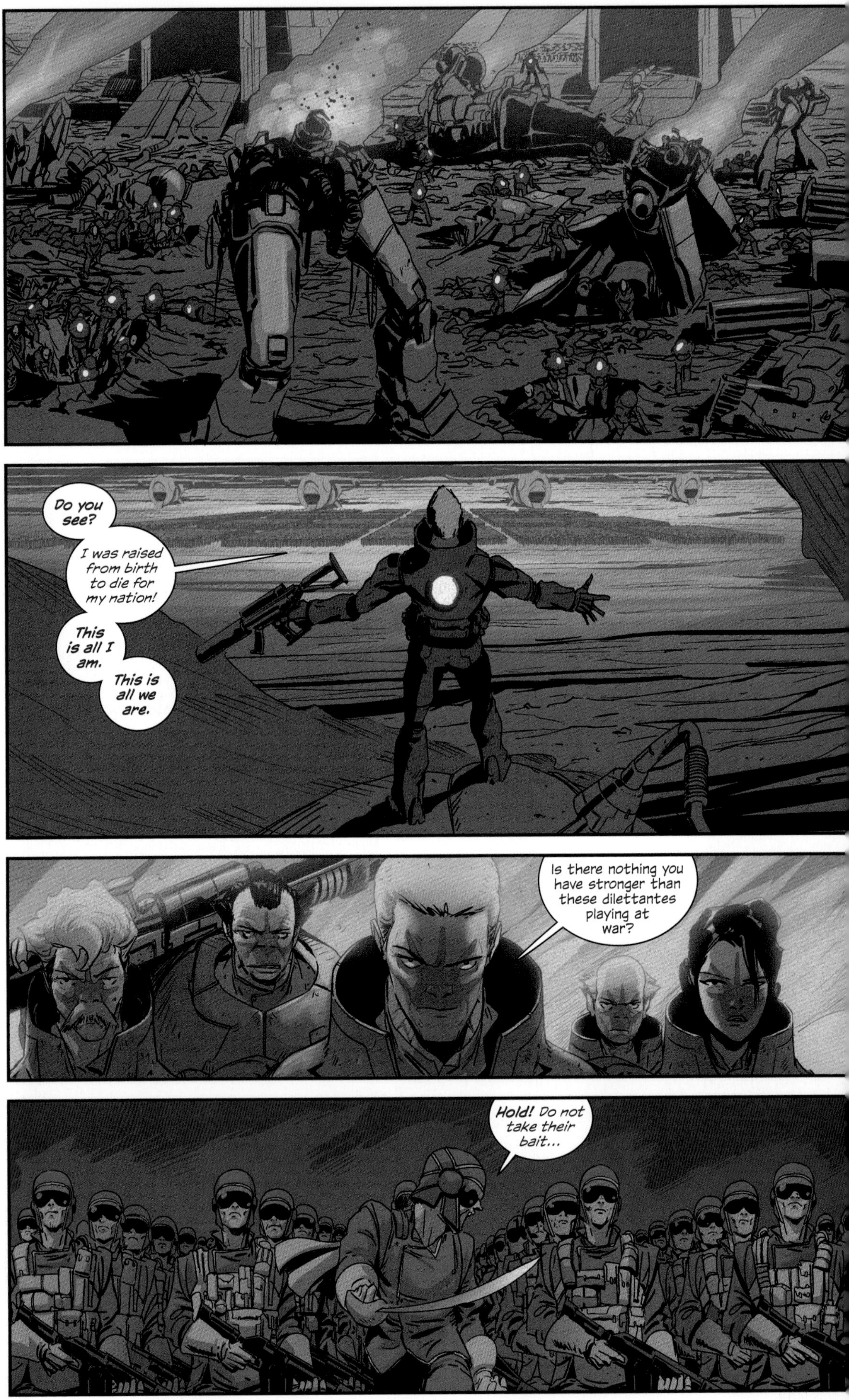
Do you see?
I was raised from birth to die for my nation!
This is all I am.
This is all we are.
Is there nothing you have stronger than these dilettantes playing at war?
Hold! Do not take their bait...

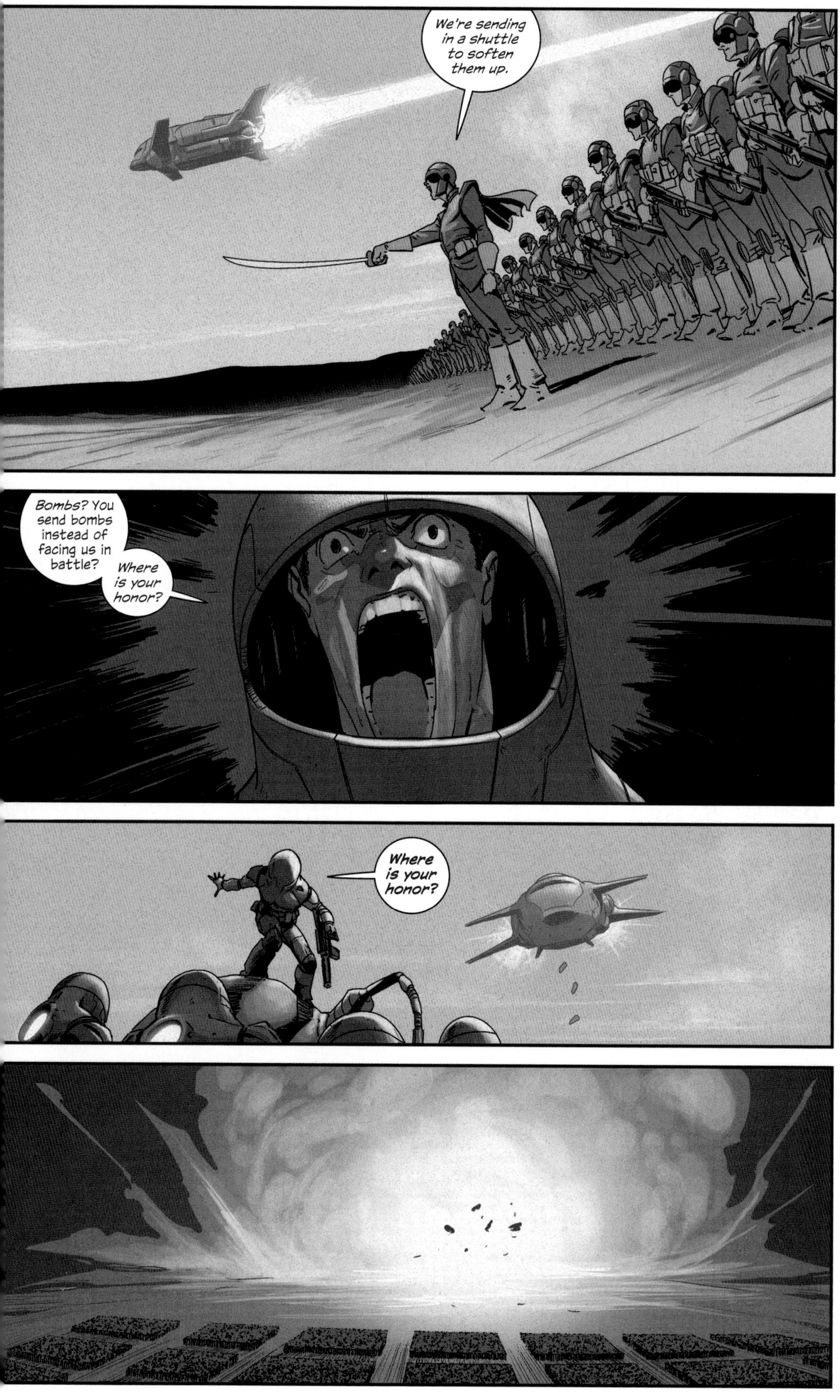
We're sending in a shuttle to soften them up.
Bombs? You send bombs instead of facing us in battle?
Where is your honor?
Where is your honor?

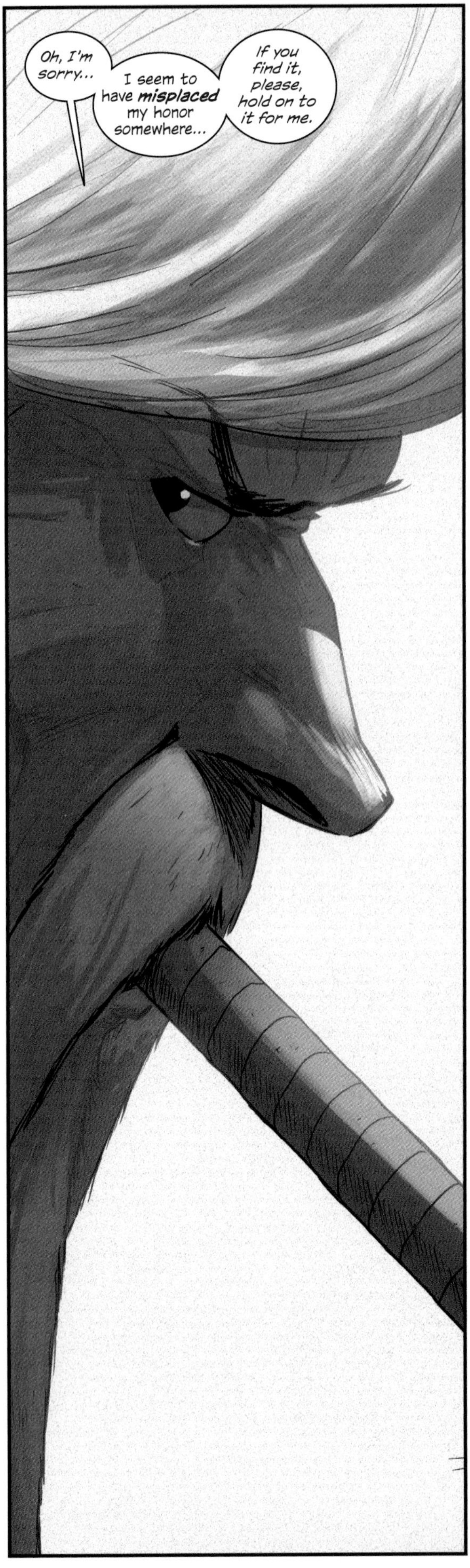
Oh, I'm sorry...
I seem to have **misplaced** my honor somewhere...
If you find it, please, hold on to it for me.

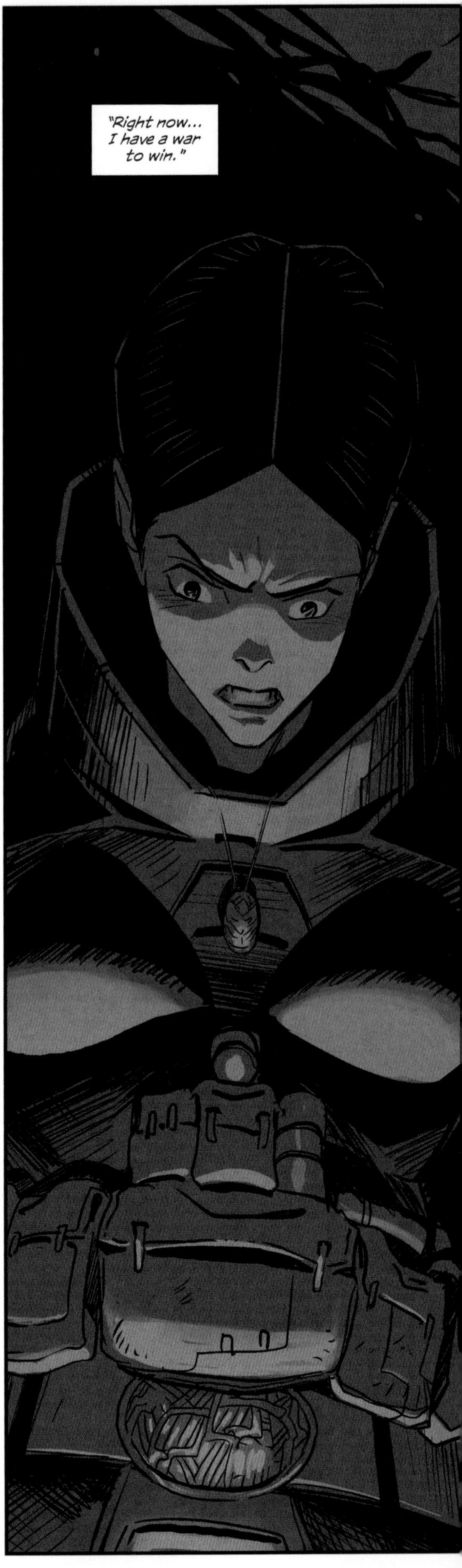
"Right now... I have a war to win."

THERE'S ONLY **ONE WAY**
THIS **ENDS...**

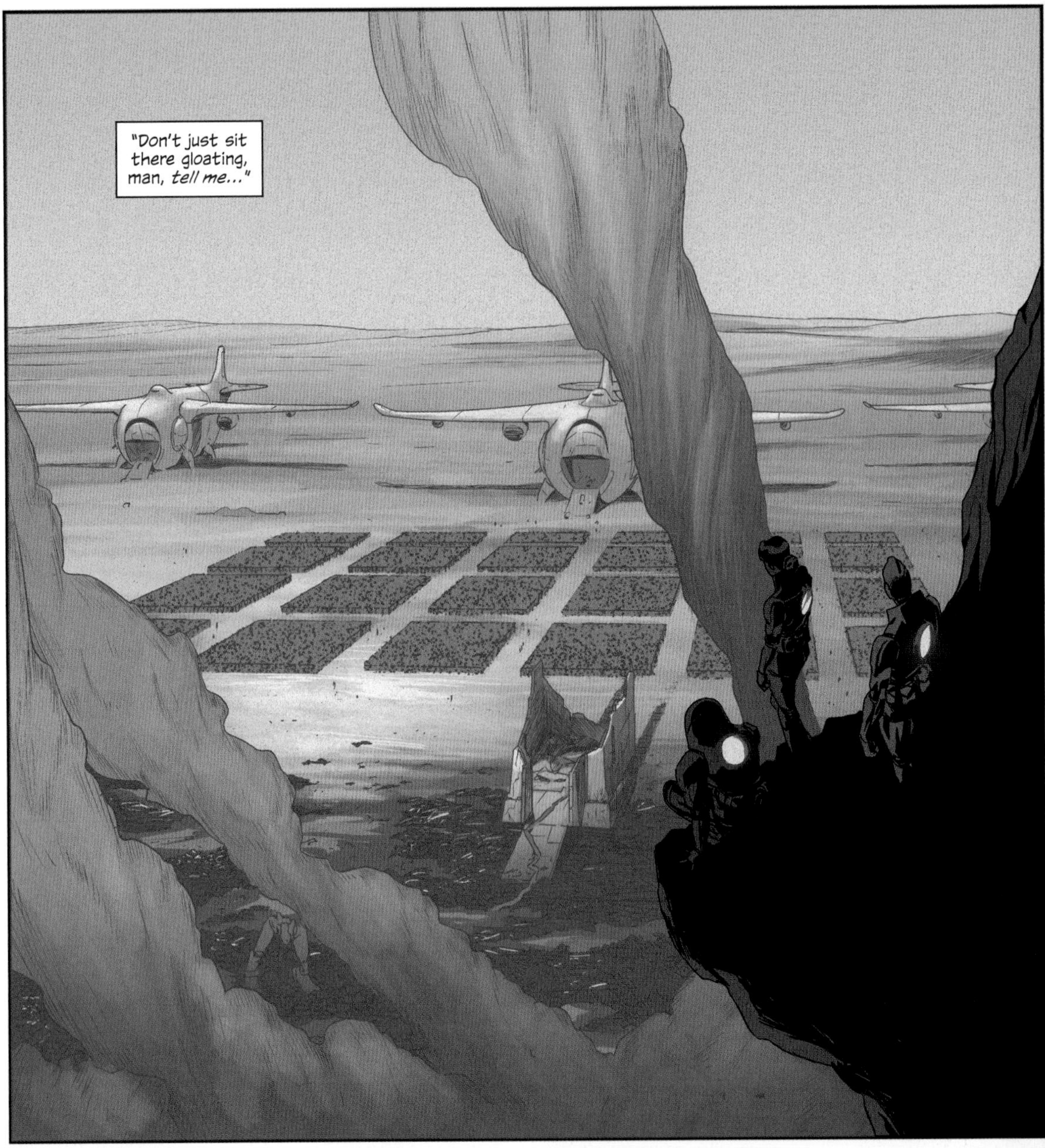
"Don't just sit there gloating, man, *tell me...*"

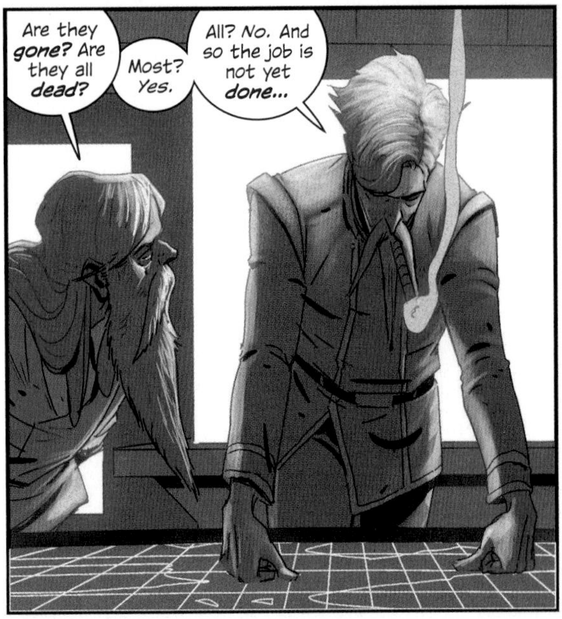
Are they **gone?** Are they all **dead?**
Most? *Yes.*
All? *No.* And so the job is not yet **done...**

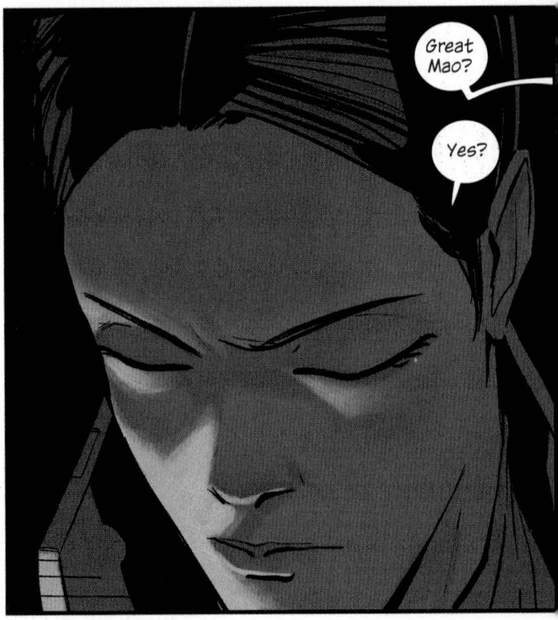
Great Mao?
Yes?

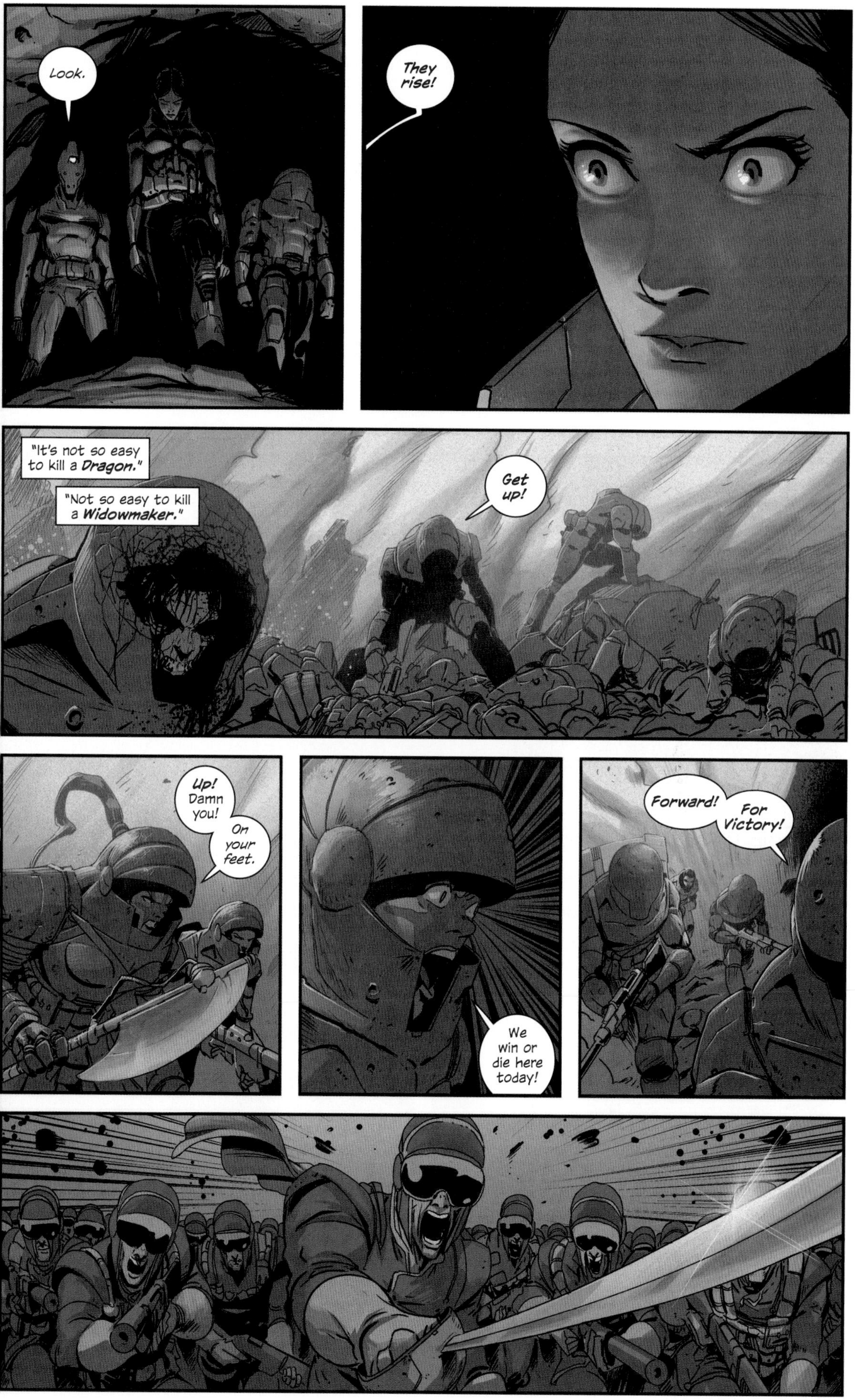
Look.
They rise!
"It's not so easy to kill a *Dragon.*"
"Not so easy to kill a *Widowmaker.*"
Get up!
Up! Damn you!
On your feet.
We win or die here today!
Forward!
For Victory!

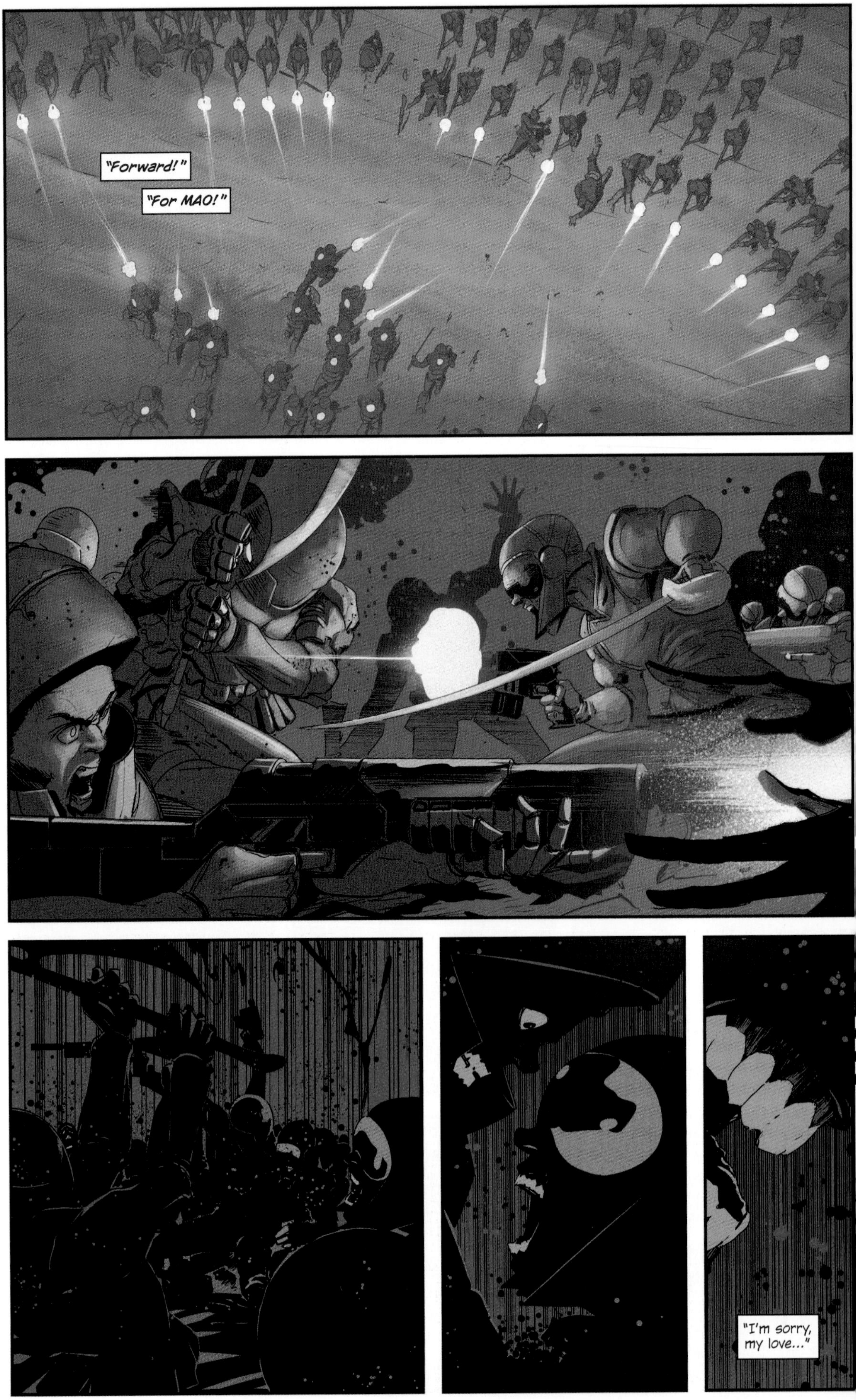
"Forward!"
"For MAO!"
"I'm sorry, my love..."

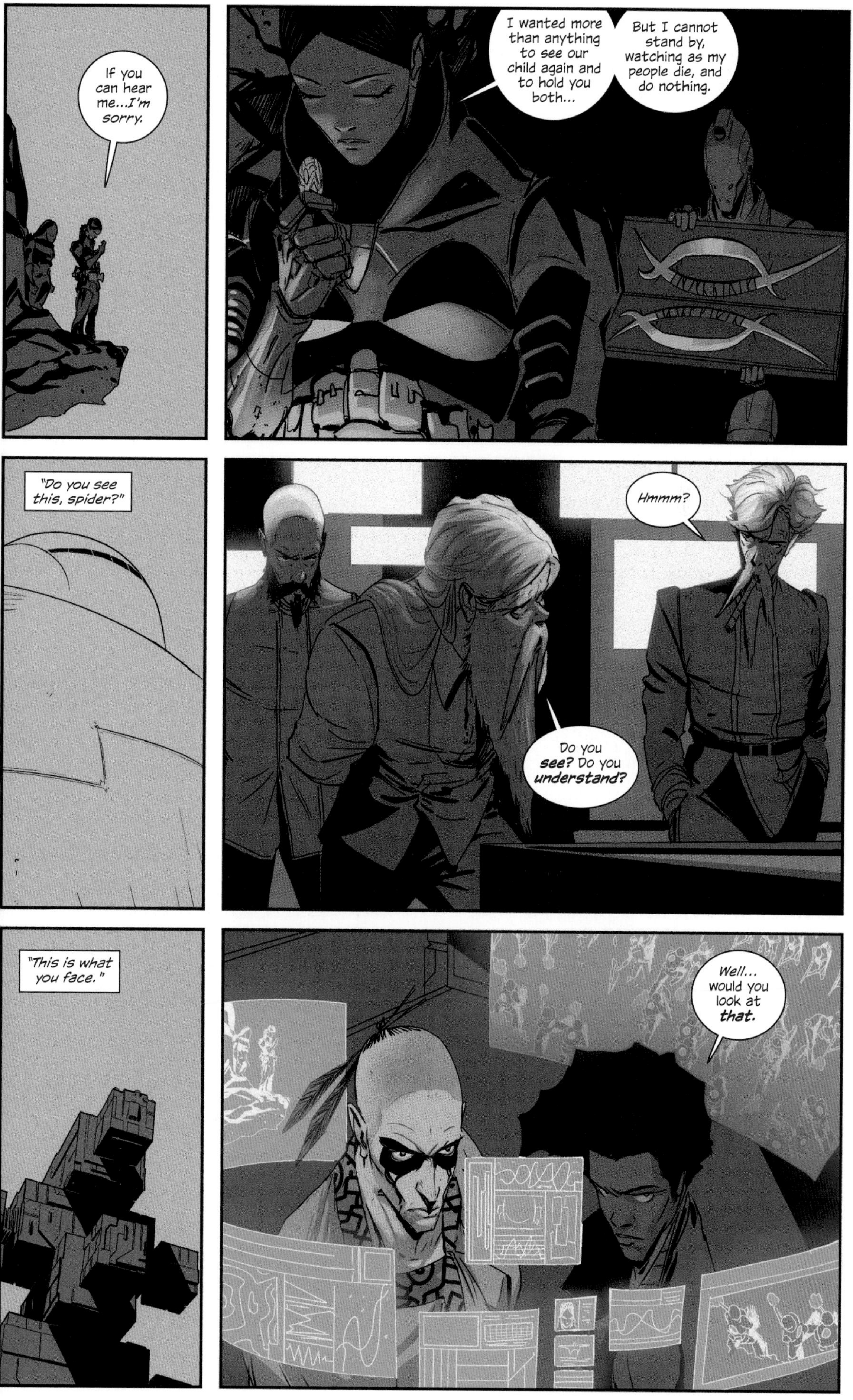
If you can hear me...I'm sorry.
I wanted more than anything to see our child again and to hold you both...
But I cannot stand by, watching as my people die, and do nothing.
"Do you see this, spider?"
Hmmm?
Do you see? Do you understand?
"This is what you face."
Well... would you look at that.

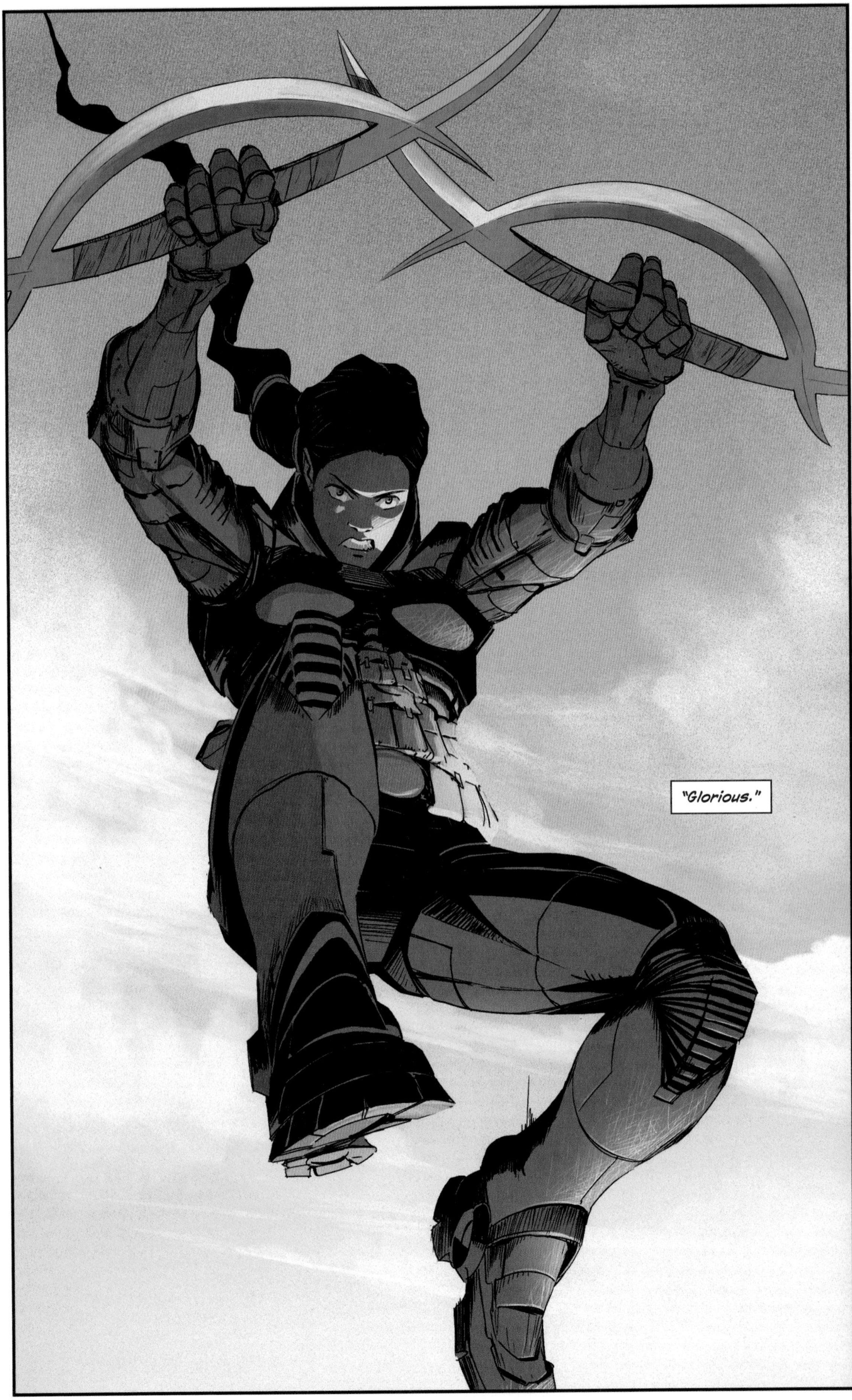
"Glorious."

ONE OF US **LIVES**, ONE
OF US **DIES.**

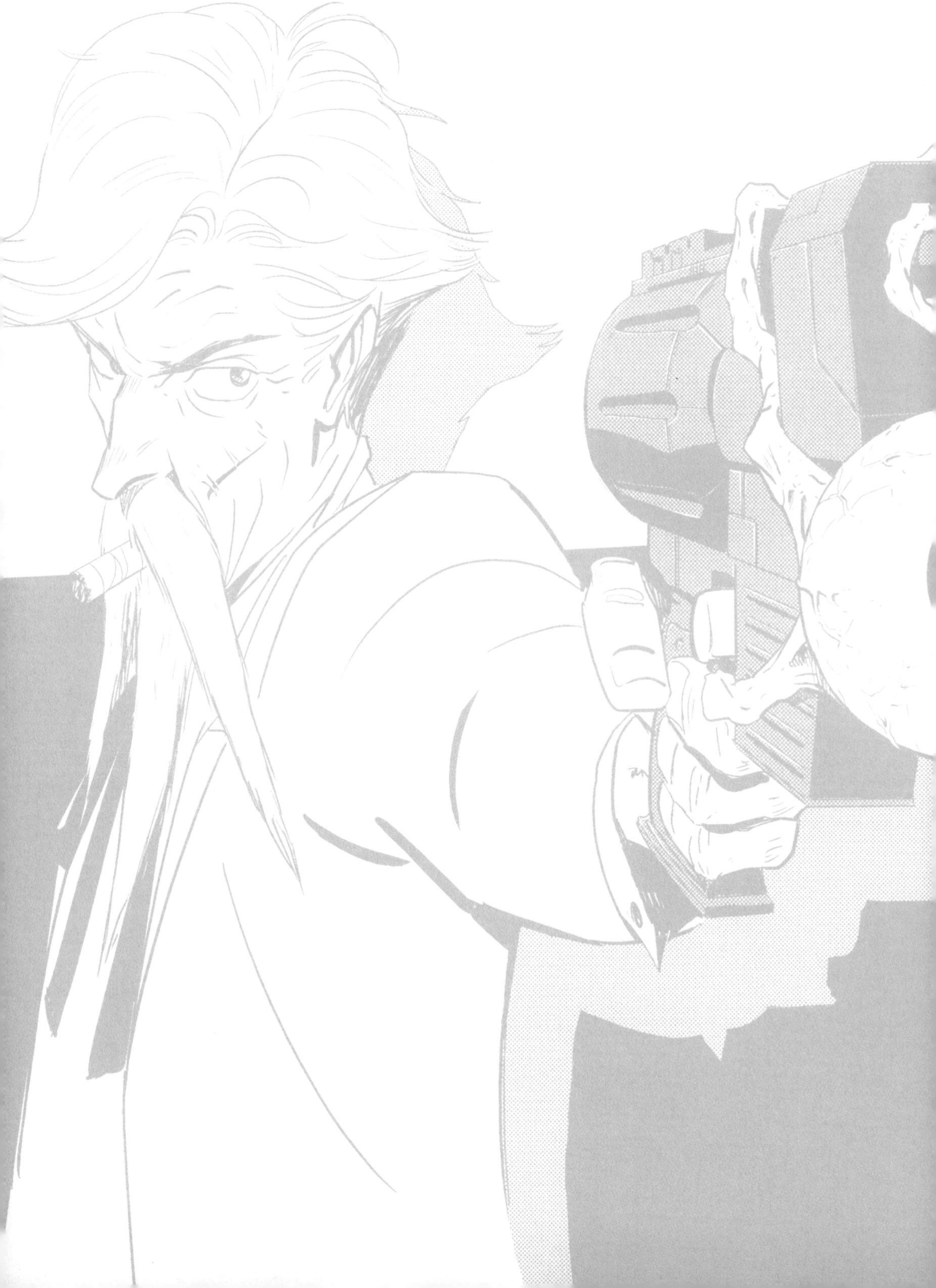

44

FORTY-FOUR:
ONE **EYE,** ONE
WINNER

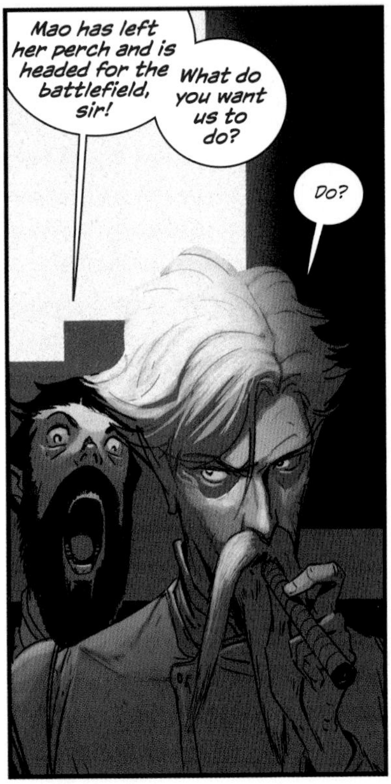
Mao has left her perch and is headed for the battlefield, sir!
What do you want us to do?
Do?

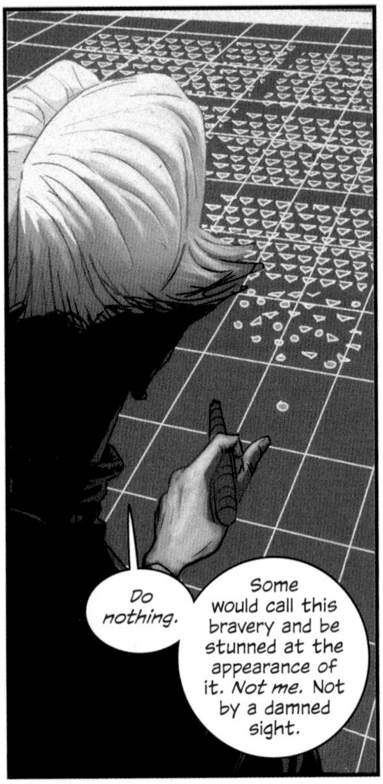
Do nothing.
Some would call this bravery and be stunned at the appearance of it. *Not me.* Not by a damned sight.

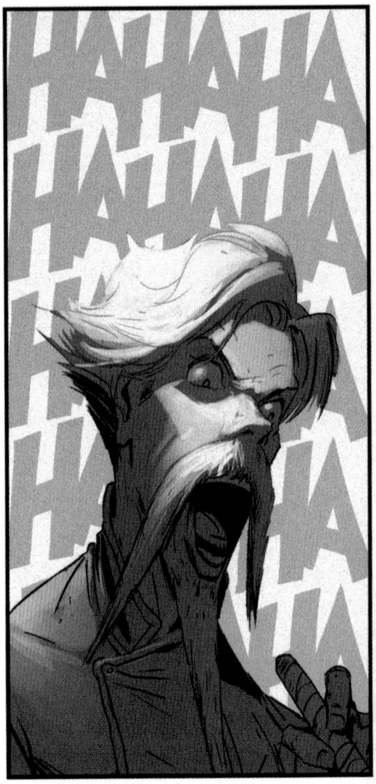
HAHAHAHAHAHAHAHAHAHAHAHAHAHAHAHA

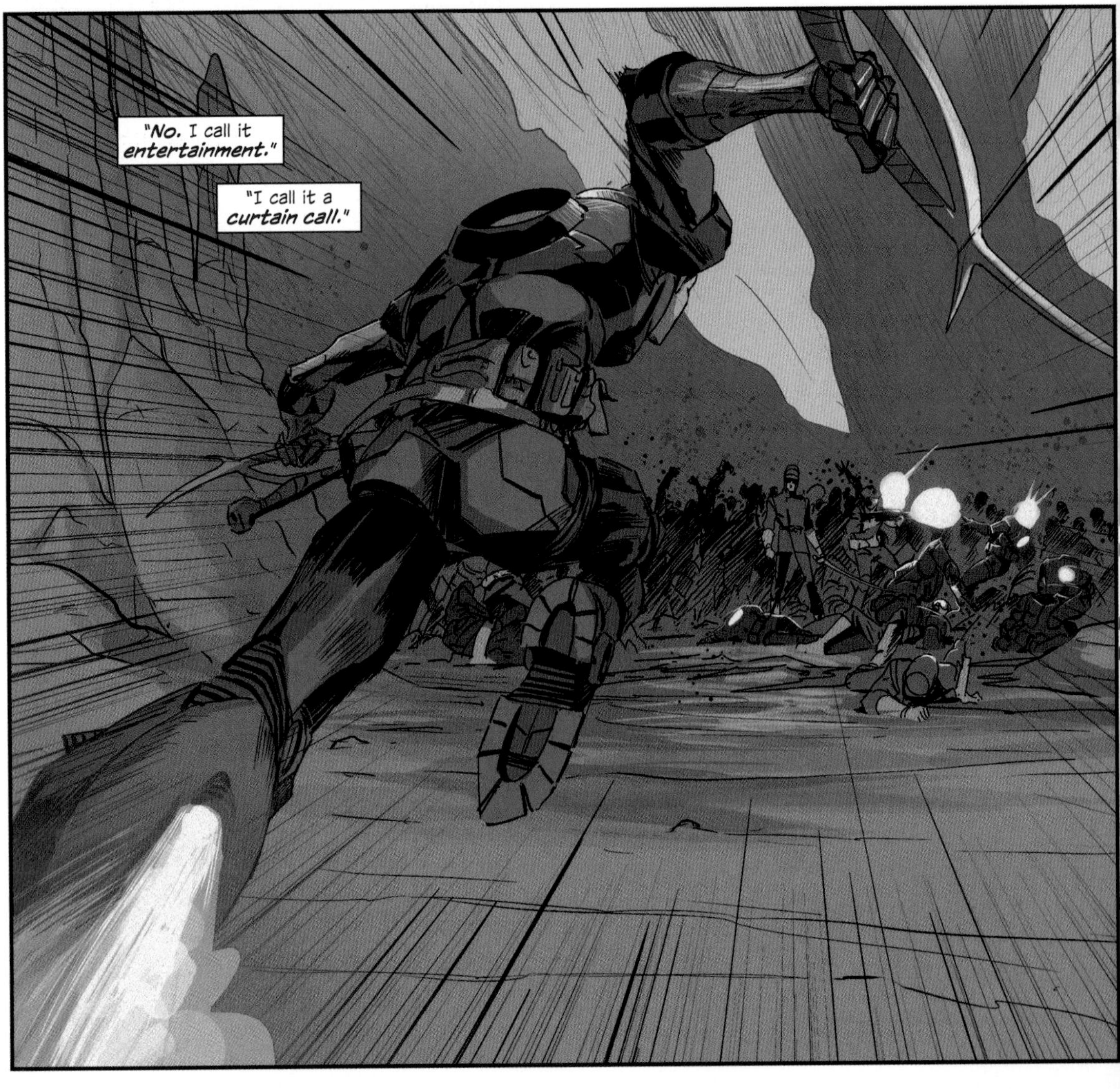
"**No.** I call it *entertainment.*"
"I call it a *curtain call.*"

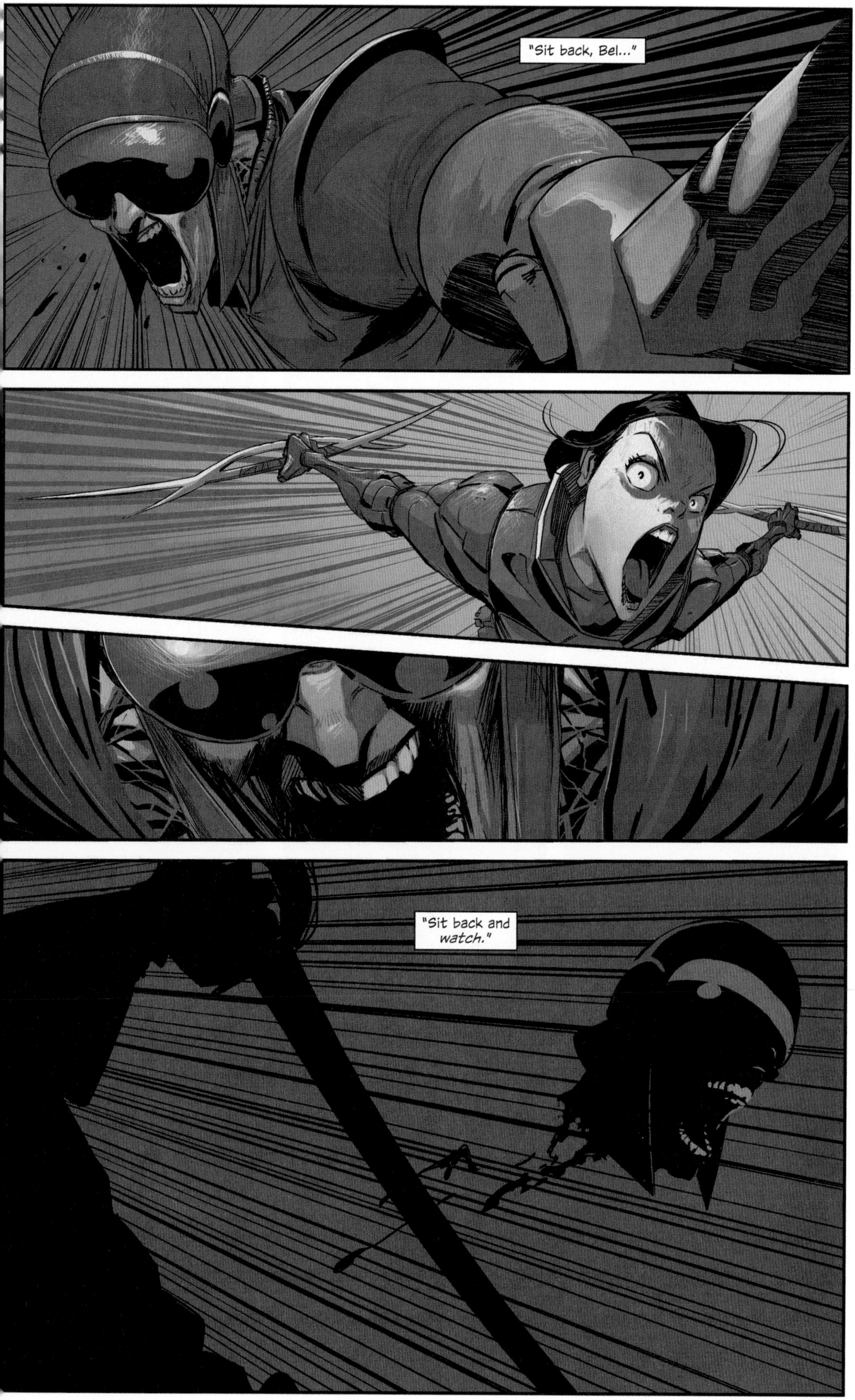
"Sit back, Bel..."
"Sit back and *watch.*"

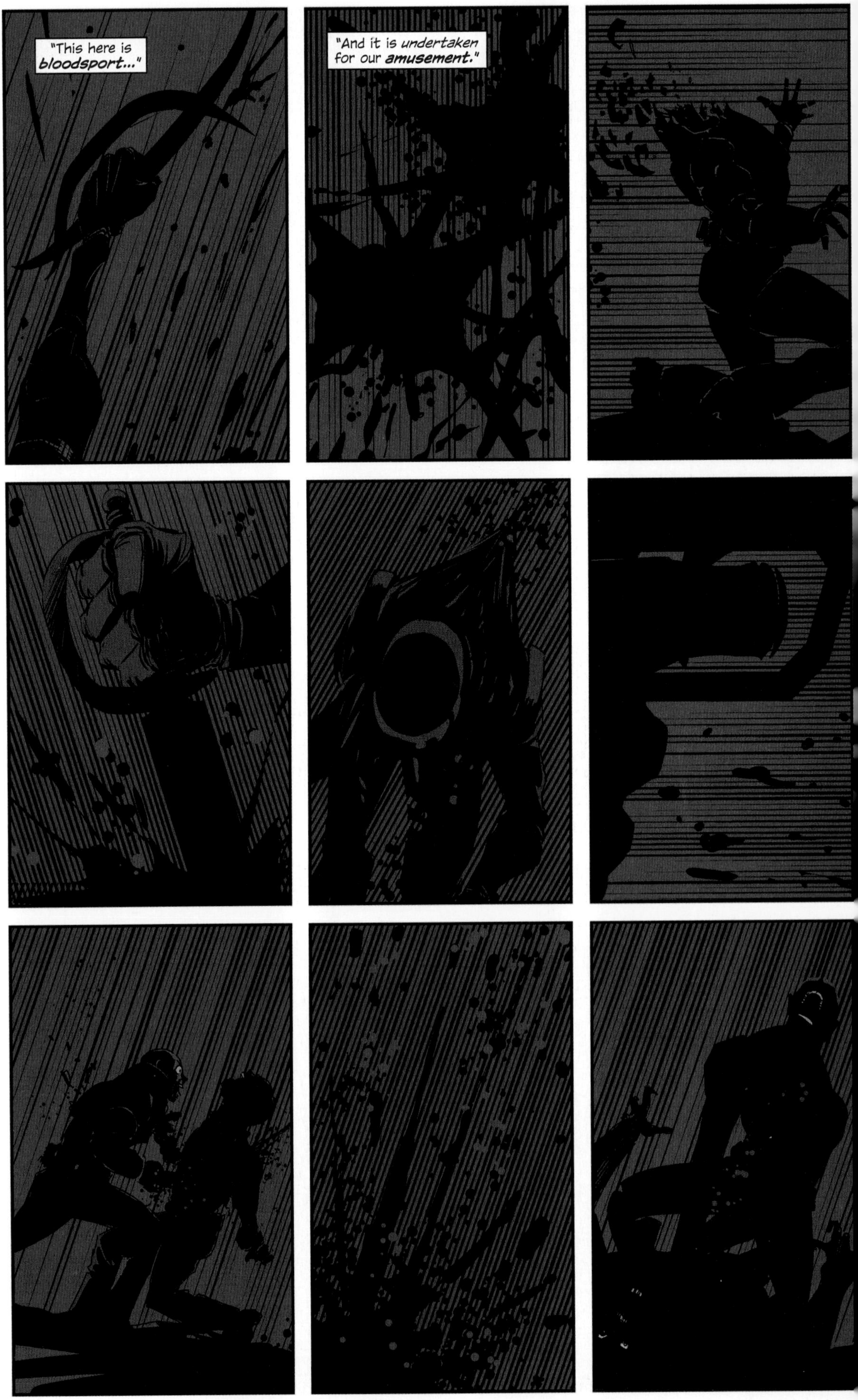
"This here is *bloodsport...*"
"And it is *undertaken* for our ***amusement.***"

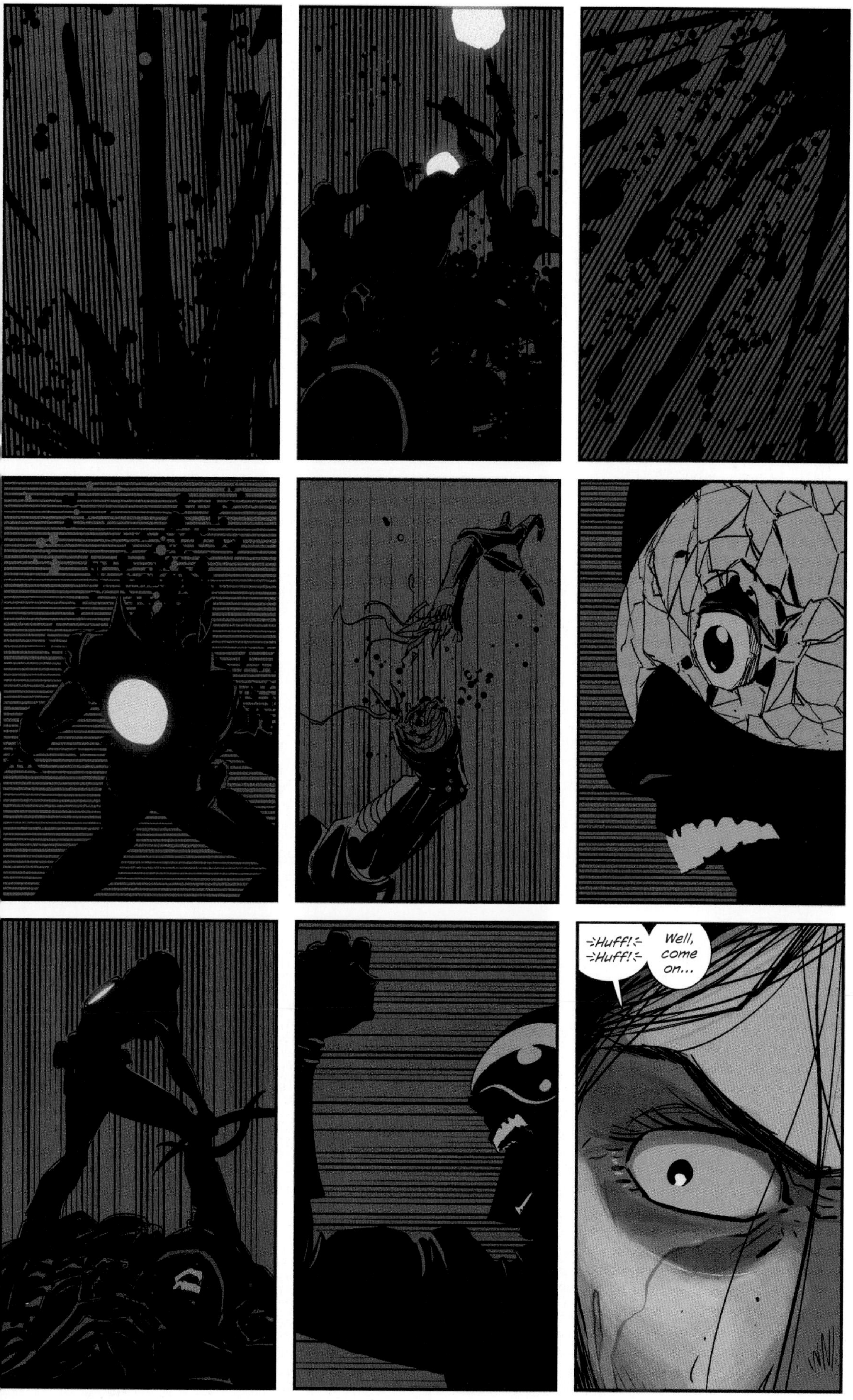

-Huff!-
-Huff!-
Well, come on...

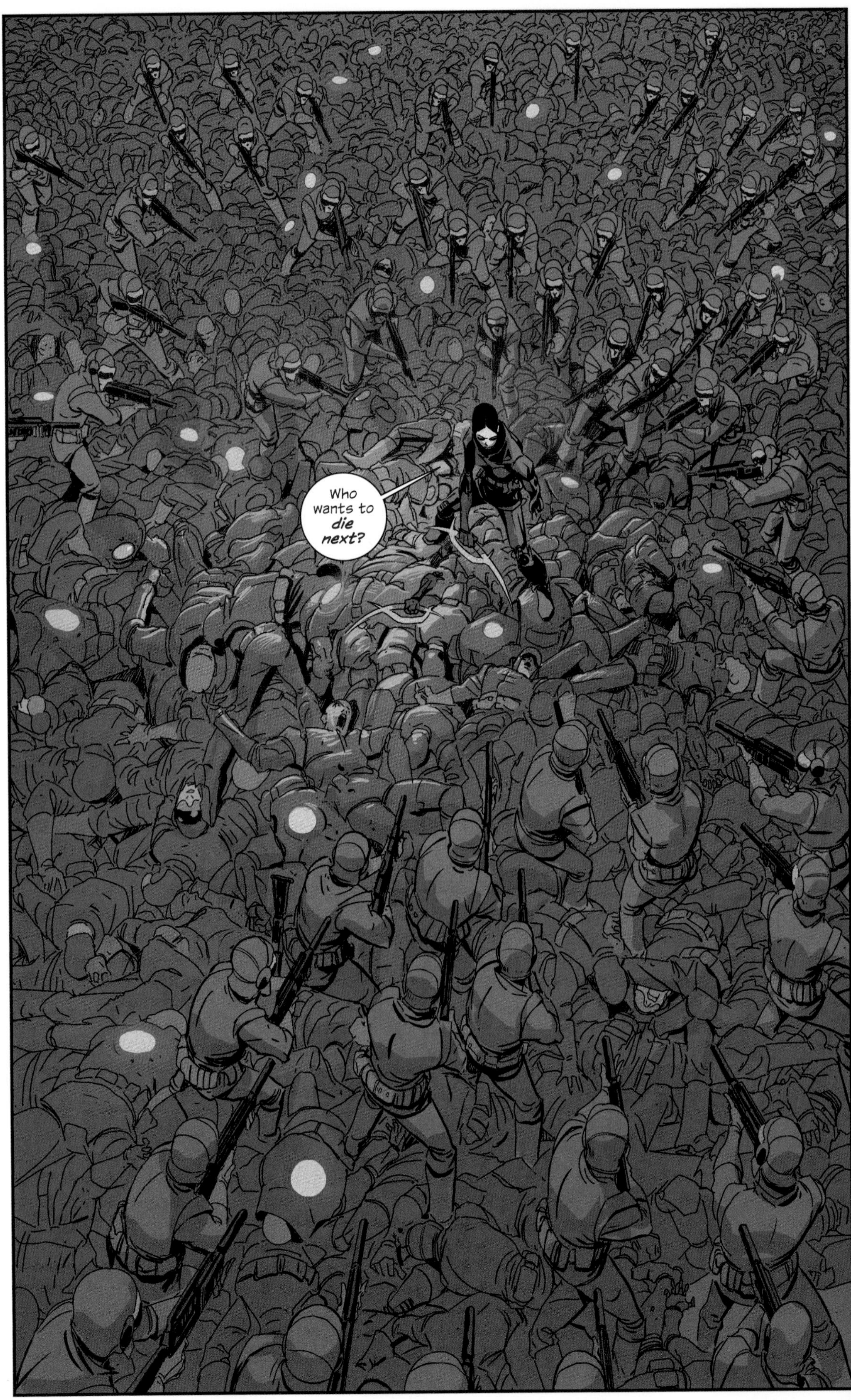
Who wants to *die next?*

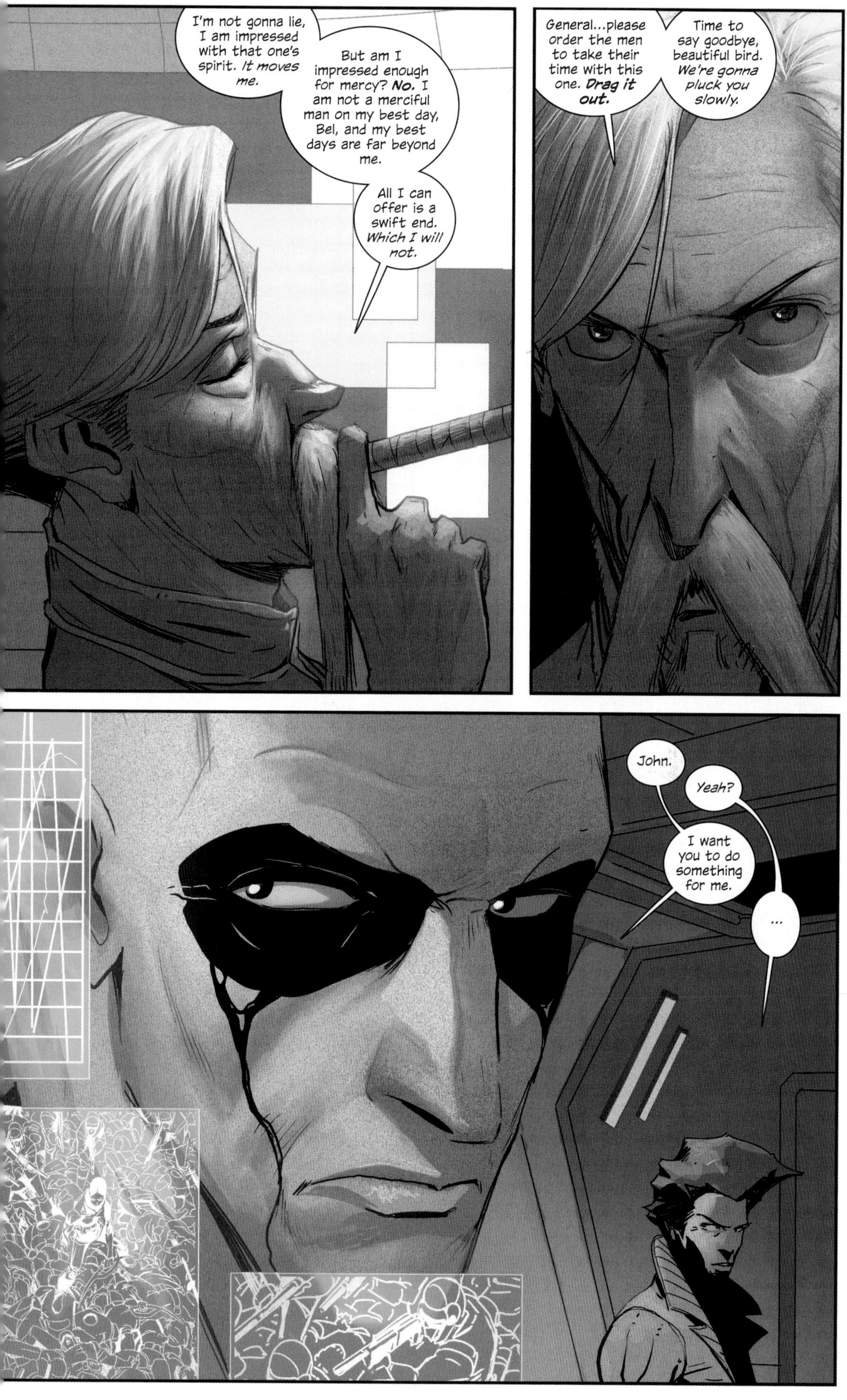
I'm not gonna lie, I am impressed with that one's spirit. *It moves me.*
But am I impressed enough for mercy? ***No.*** I am not a merciful man on my best day, Bel, and my best days are far beyond me.
All I can offer is a swift end. *Which I will not.*
General...please order the men to take their time with this one. ***Drag it out.***
Time to say goodbye, beautiful bird. *We're gonna pluck you slowly.*
John.
Yeah?
I want you to do something for me.
...

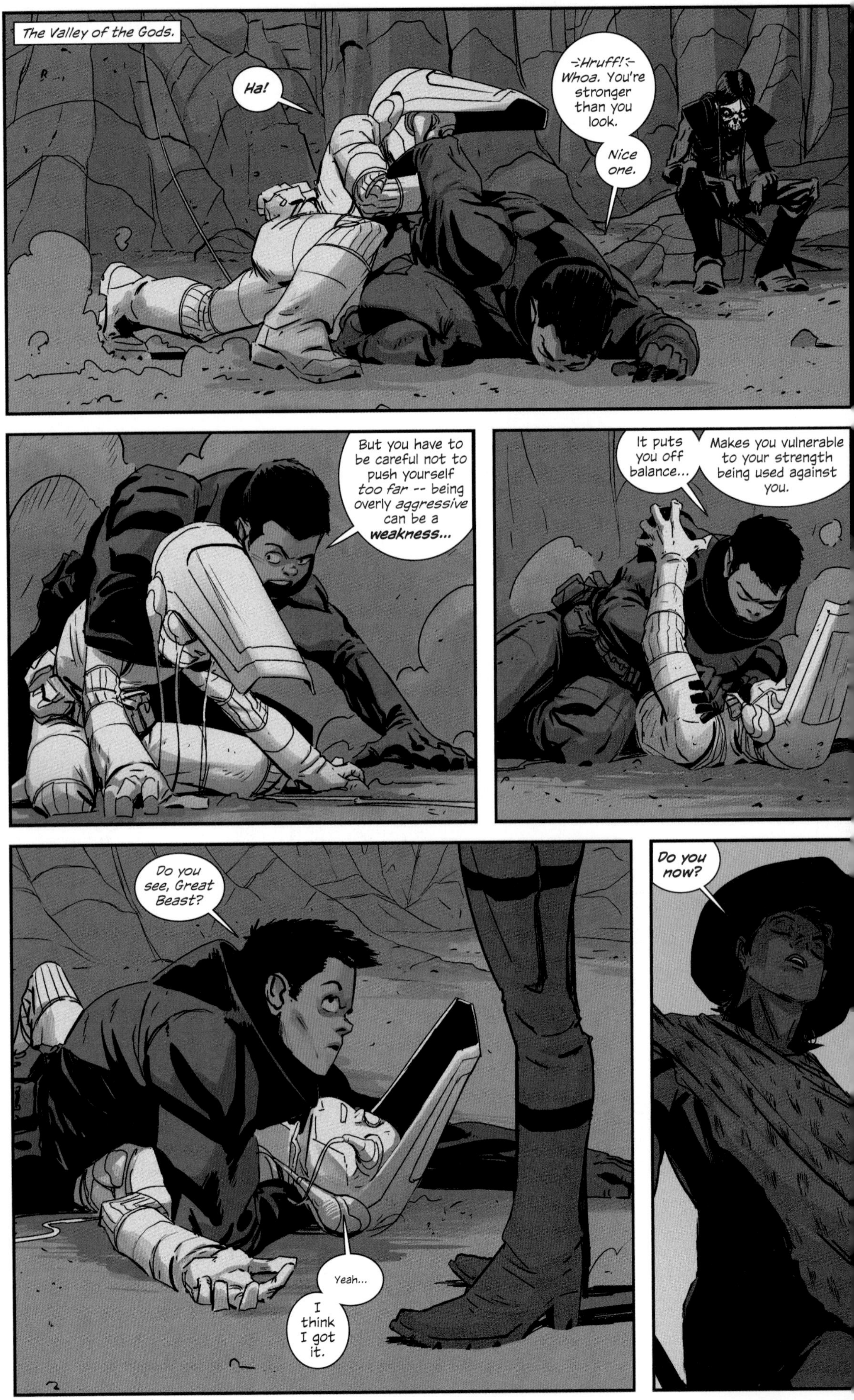
The Valley of the Gods.
Ha!
-Hruff!- Whoa. You're stronger than you look.
Nice one.
But you have to be careful not to push yourself too far -- being overly aggressive can be a weakness...
It puts you off balance...
Makes you vulnerable to your strength being used against you.
Do you see, Great Beast?
Yeah...
I think I got it.
Do you now?

Then I guess that means you understand...

You're the manifestation of Death pushing himself too far.

You're his **weakness**... and you'll be his **undoing**.

I guess that's **one way** to look at it.

I can think of **another**.

You have to see this place is a killing field.

Oh, I can see more than that.

Tell him what he's won, Balloon.

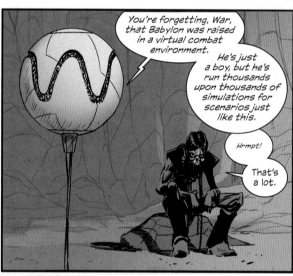

You're forgetting, War, that Babylon was raised in a virtual combat environment. He's just a boy, but he's run thousands upon thousands of simulations for scenarios just like this.

Hrmpt!

That's a lot.

It's legion, and worth remembering...

He's the **Great Beast**.

Why don't you ask him what we should do?

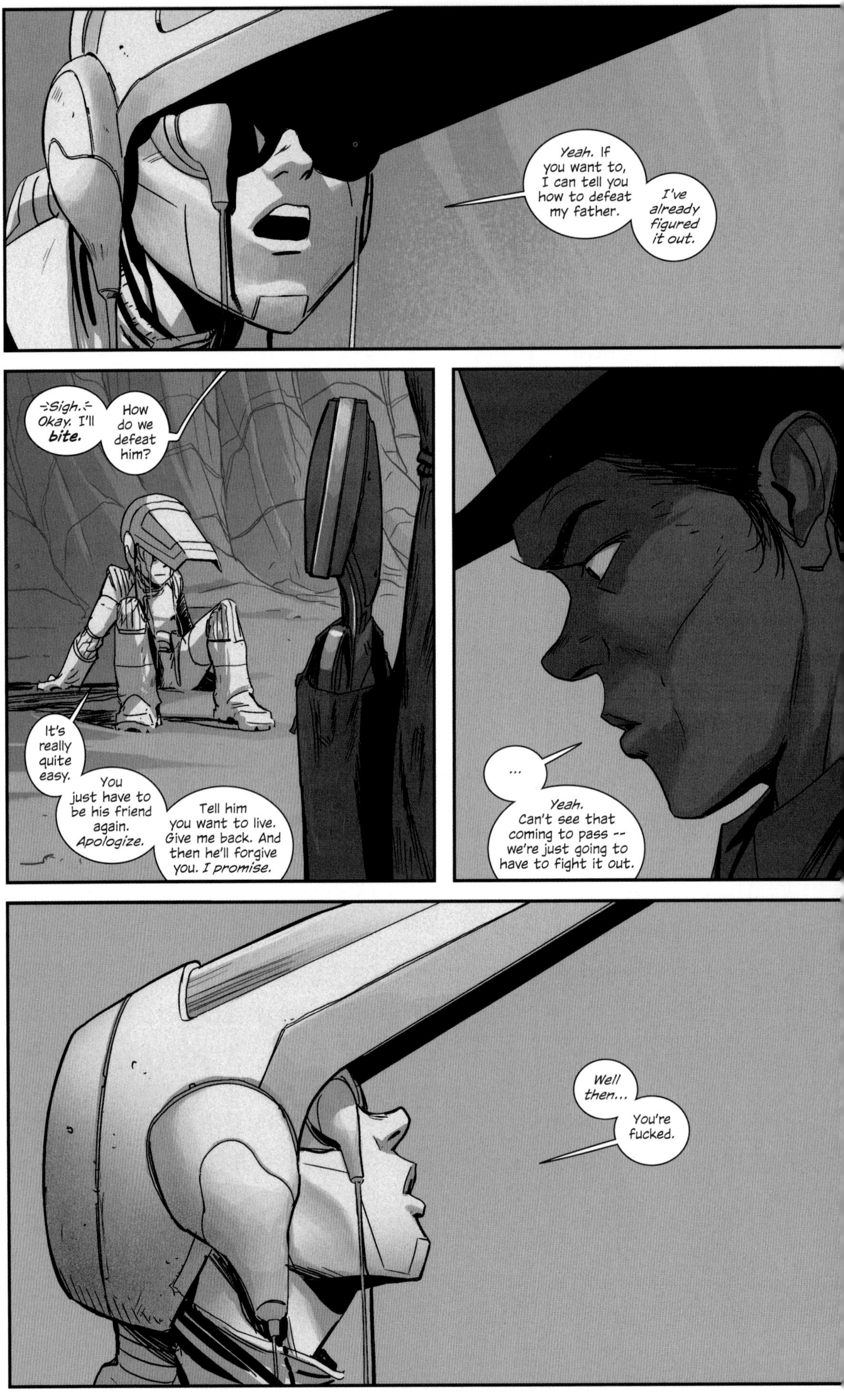
Yeah. If you want to, I can tell you how to defeat my father.
I've already figured it out.
-Sigh.- Okay. I'll bite.
How do we defeat him?
It's really quite easy.
You just have to be his friend again. Apologize.
Tell him you want to live. Give me back. And then he'll forgive you. I promise.
...
Yeah. Can't see that coming to pass -- we're just going to have to fight it out.
Well then...
You're fucked.

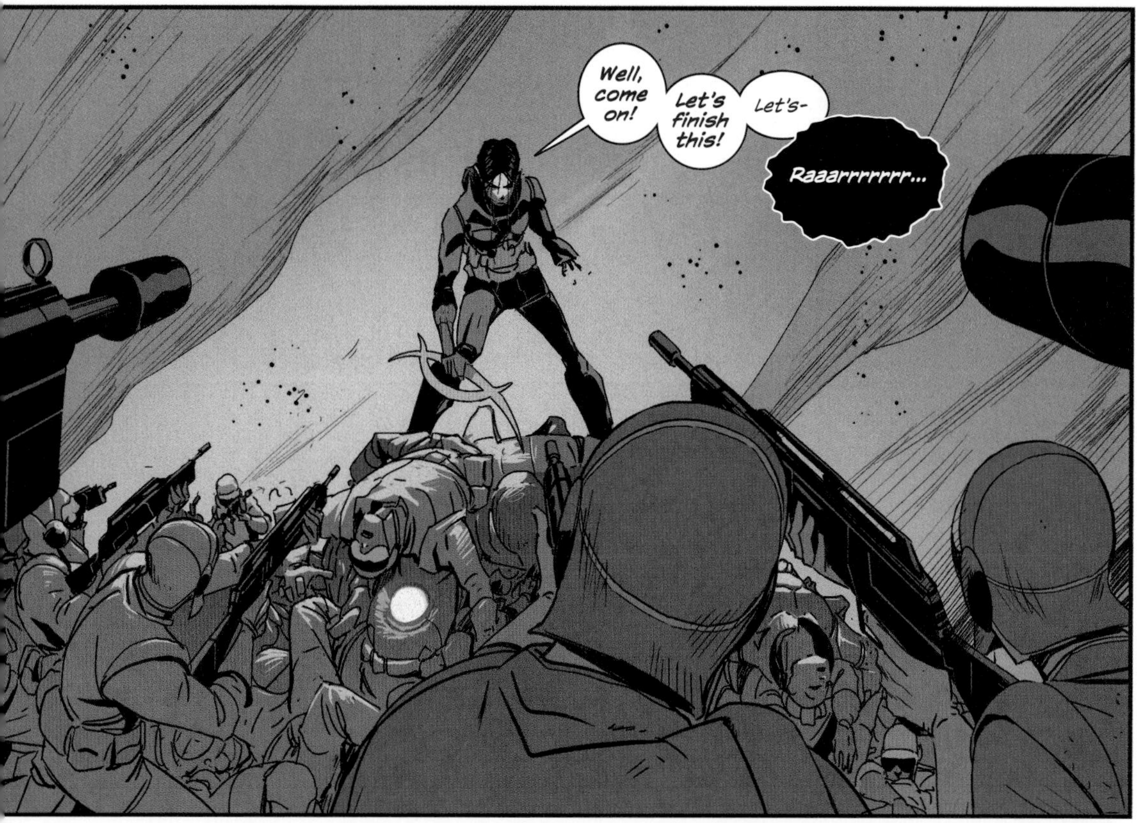
Well, come on!
Let's finish this!
Let's-
Raaarrrrrrr...

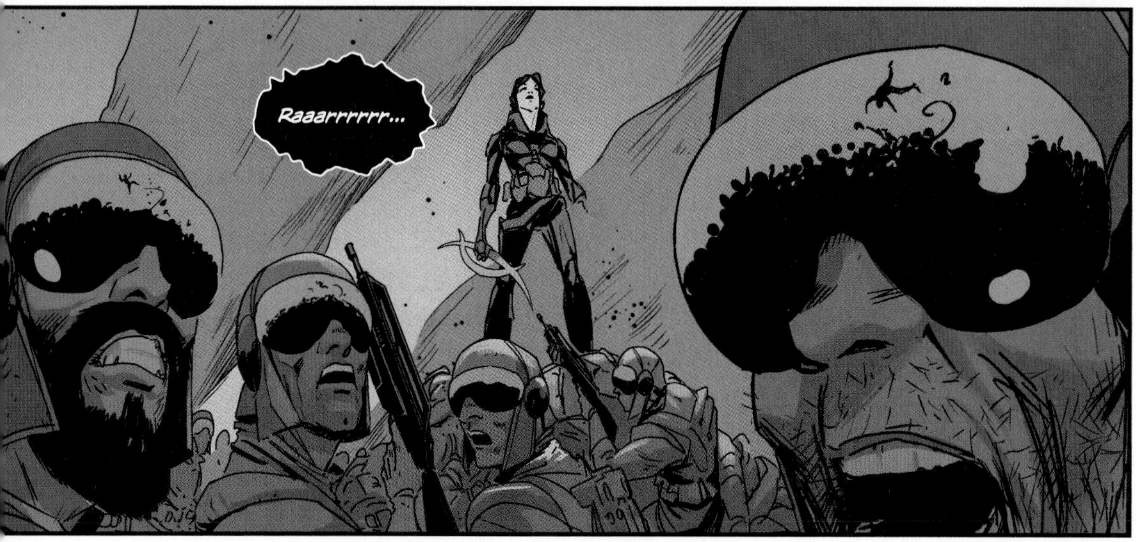
Raaarrrrrr...

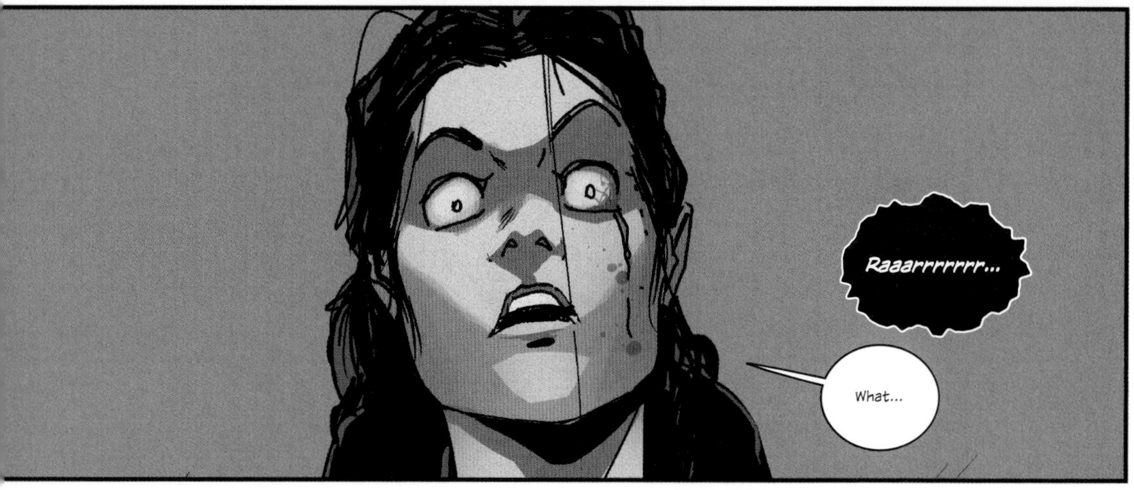
Raaarrrrrrr...
What...

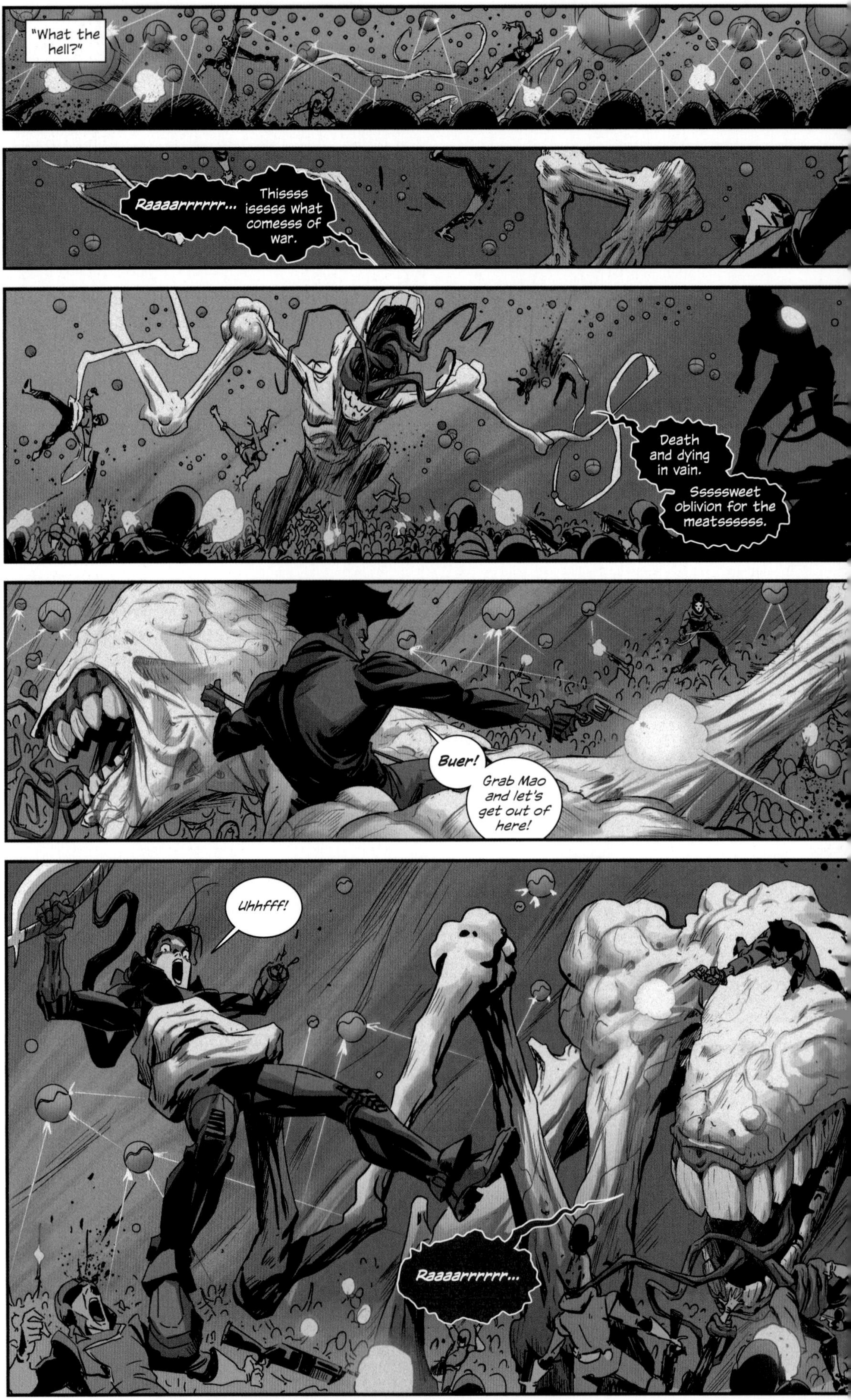
"What the hell?"
Raaaarrrrrr...
Thissss isssss what comesss of war.
Death and dying in vain.
Sssssweet oblivion for the meatssssss.
Buer!
Grab Mao and let's get out of here!
Uhhfff!
Raaaarrrrrr...

Hold on tight.

Buer's a bit slippery.

Raaaarrrrr...

Not sssssslippery... **sssssslimy...** there'sssss a difference.

Why...

Why'd you save me?

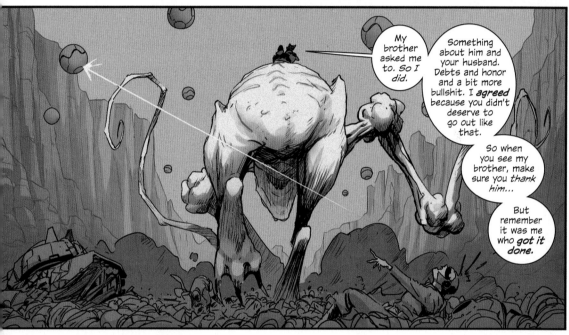

My brother asked me to. So I did.

Something about him and your husband. Debts and honor and a bit more bullshit. I *agreed* because you didn't deserve to go out like that.

So when you see my brother, make sure you *thank him...*

But remember it was me who **got it done.**

They've escaped with Xiaolian, sir! But all her remaining forces have been defeated. Completely.

Should we pursue?

Chase after them?

To what end?

I thought killing her slow would be the worst thing I could do to her...

But now that I ponder my predicament in a more thorough fashion -- let her live with being a queen of nothing. *It suits her.*

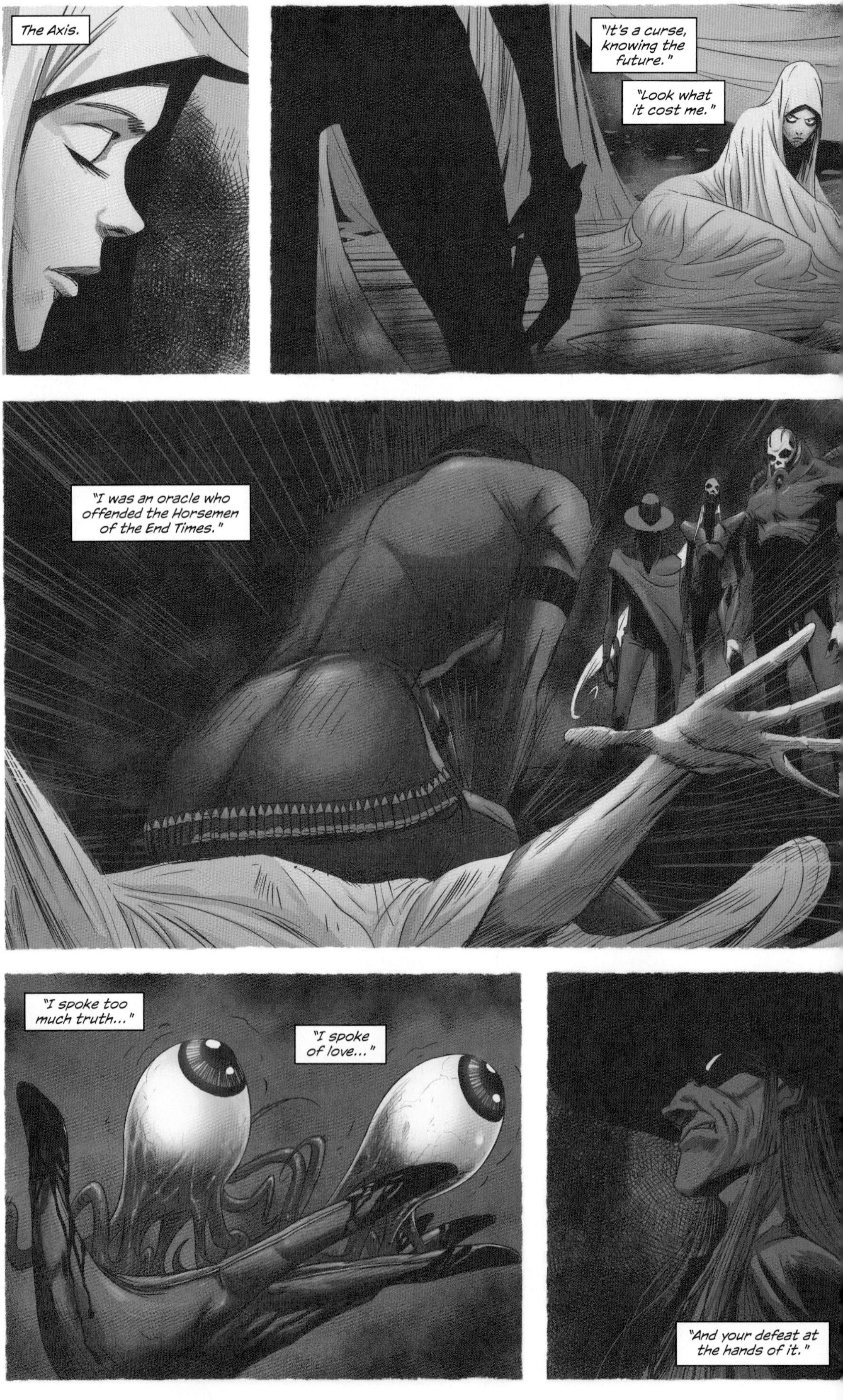
The Axis.
"It's a curse, knowing the future."
"Look what it cost me."
"I was an oracle who offended the Horsemen of the End Times."
"I spoke too much truth..."
"I spoke of love..."
"And your defeat at the hands of it."

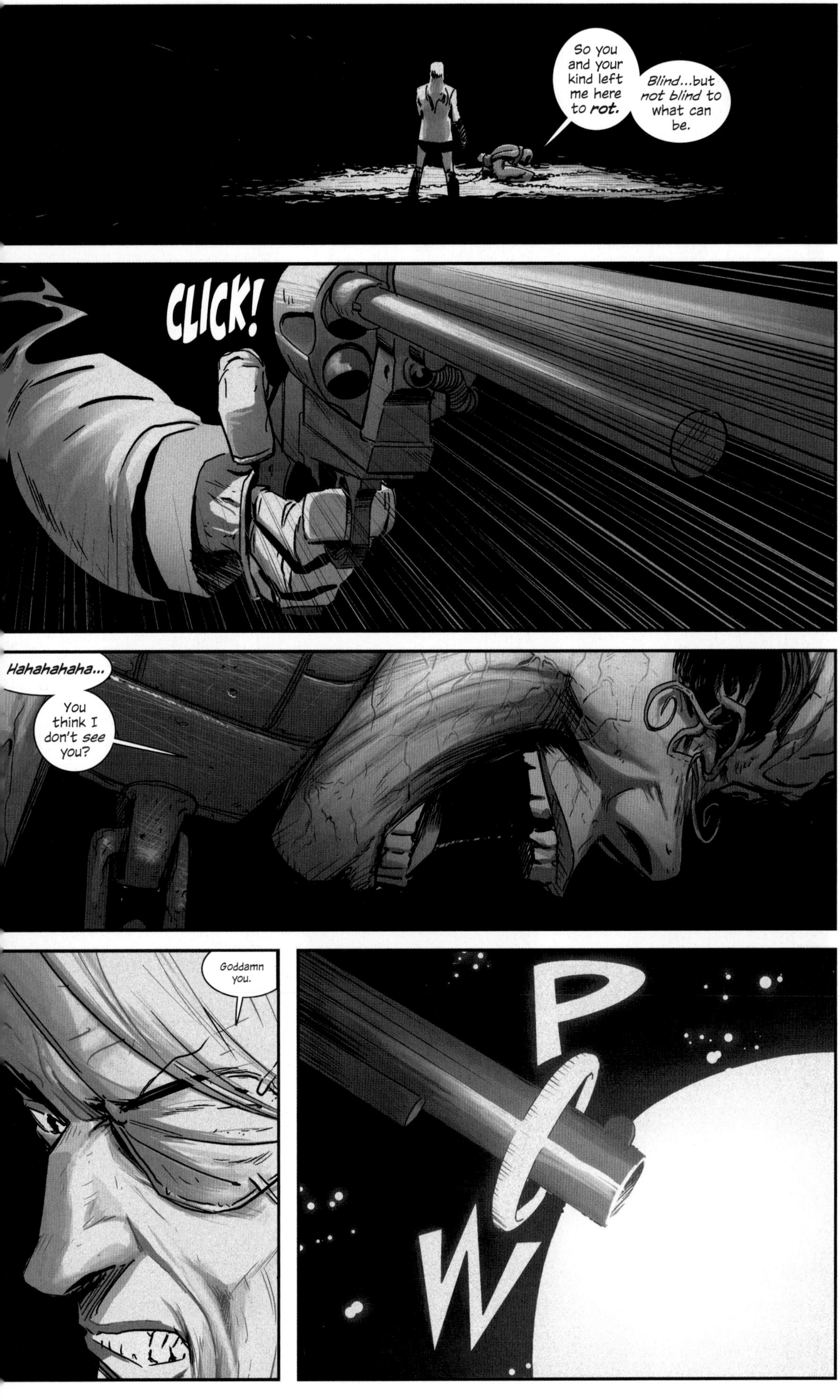

So you and your kind left me here to *rot.*
Blind...but *not blind* to what can be.
CLICK!
Hahahahaha...
You think I don't see you?
Goddamn you.
POW

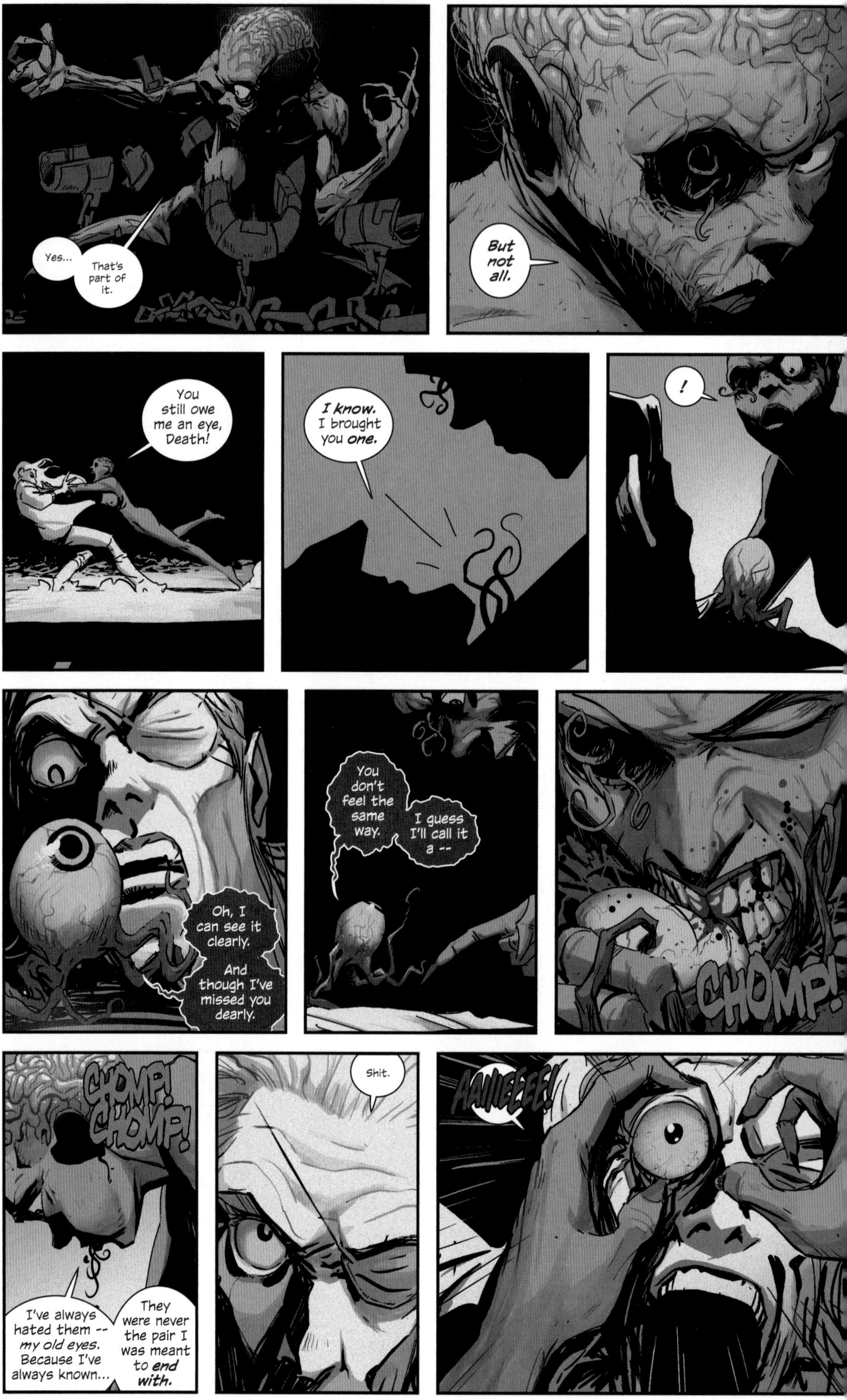
Yes...
That's part of it.
But not all.
You still owe me an eye, Death!
I know. I brought you one.
!
Oh, I can see it clearly.
And though I've missed you dearly.
You don't feel the same way.
I guess I'll call it a --
CHOMP!
CHOMP! CHOMP!
I've always hated them -- my old eyes. Because I've always known...
They were never the pair I was meant to end with.
Shit.
AAIIIEEEE!

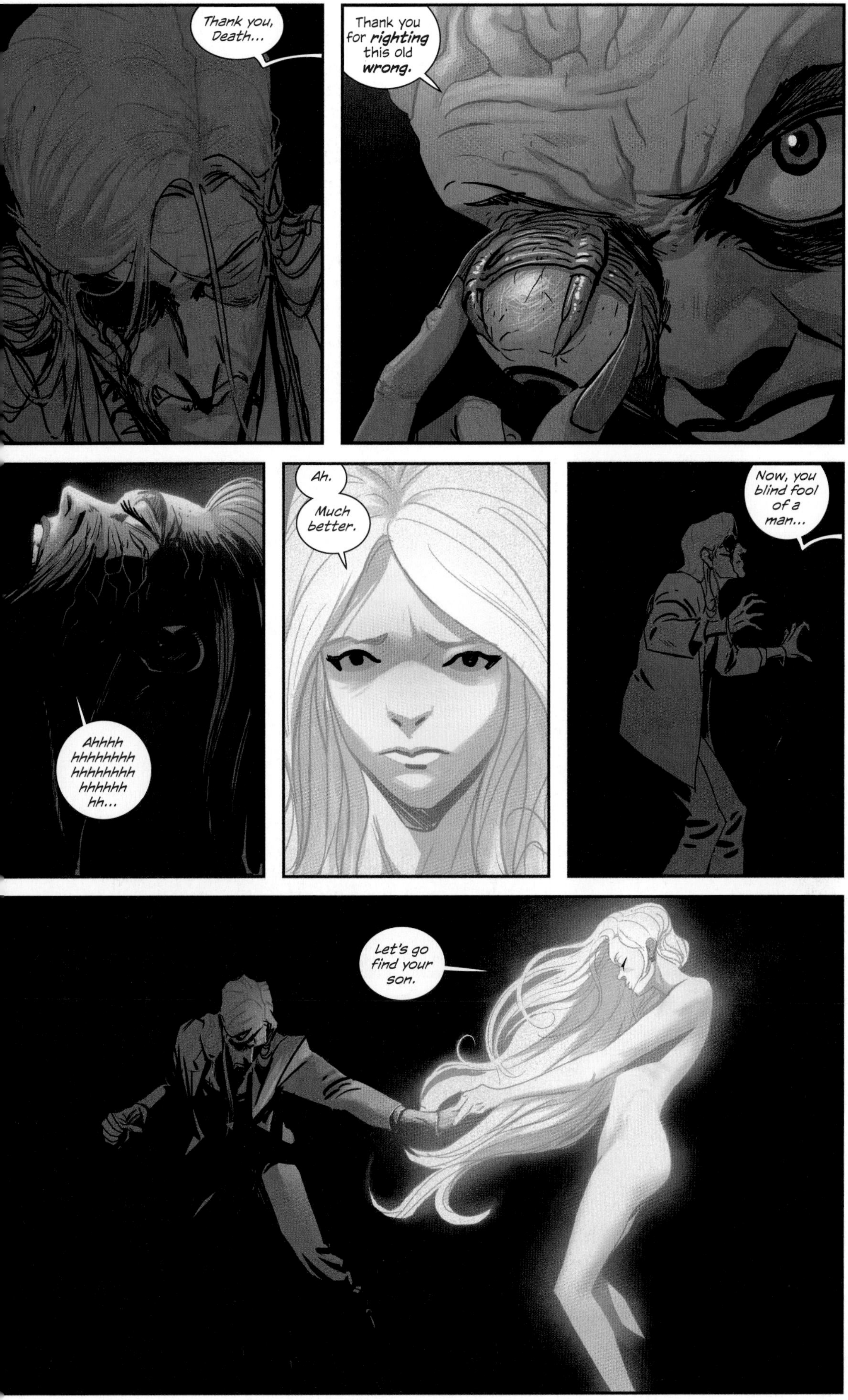
Thank you, Death...
Thank you for righting this old wrong.
Ahhhh hhhhhhhh hhhhhhhh hhhhhh hh...
Ah.
Much better.
Now, you blind fool of a man...
Let's go find your son.

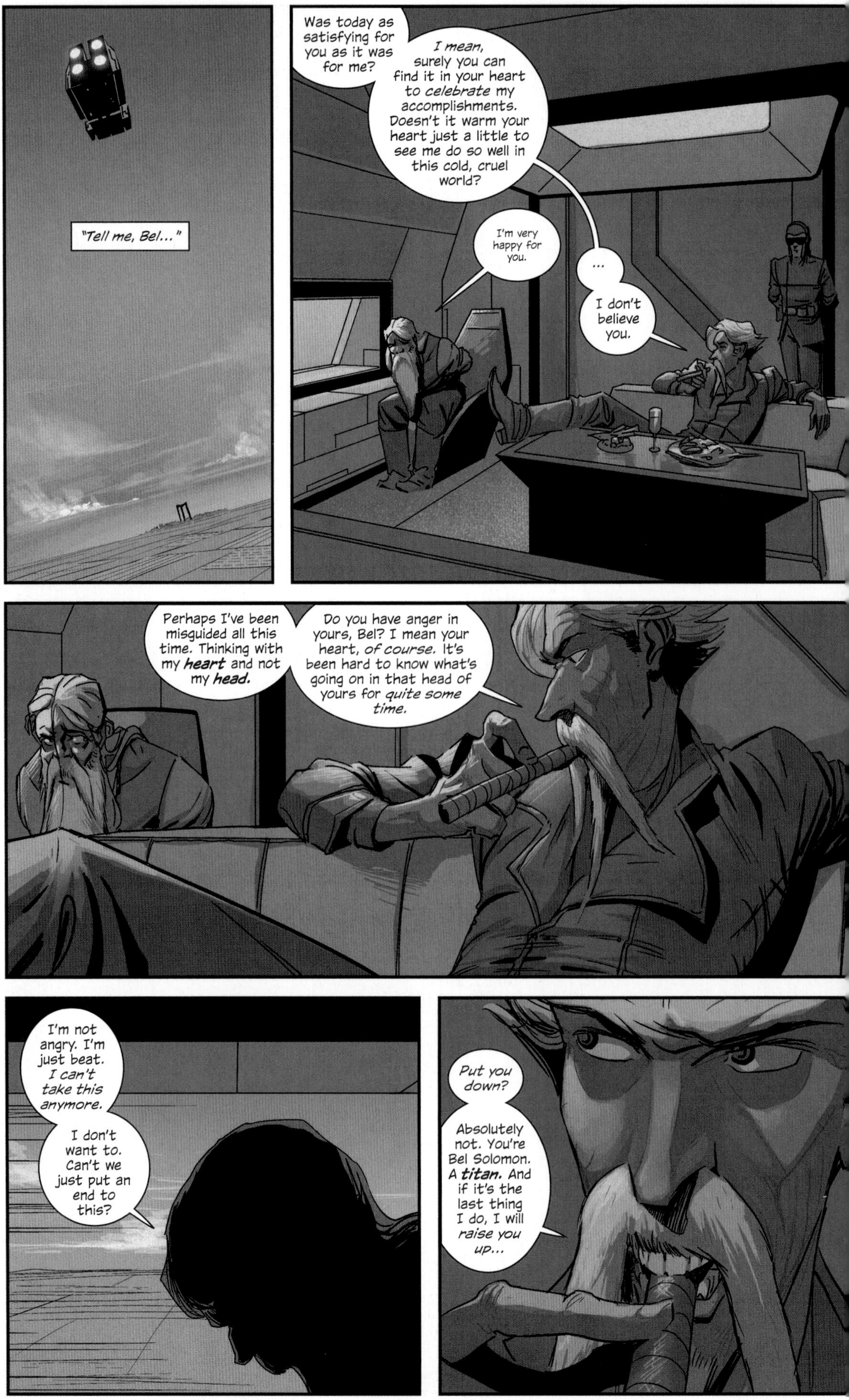
"Tell me, Bel..."
Was today as satisfying for you as it was for me?
I mean, surely you can find it in your heart to celebrate my accomplishments. Doesn't it warm your heart just a little to see me do so well in this cold, cruel world?
I'm very happy for you.
...
I don't believe you.
Perhaps I've been misguided all this time. Thinking with my heart and not my head.
Do you have anger in yours, Bel? I mean your heart, of course. It's been hard to know what's going on in that head of yours for quite some time.
I'm not angry. I'm just beat. I can't take this anymore.
I don't want to. Can't we just put an end to this?
Put you down?
Absolutely not. You're Bel Solomon. A titan. And if it's the last thing I do, I will raise you up...

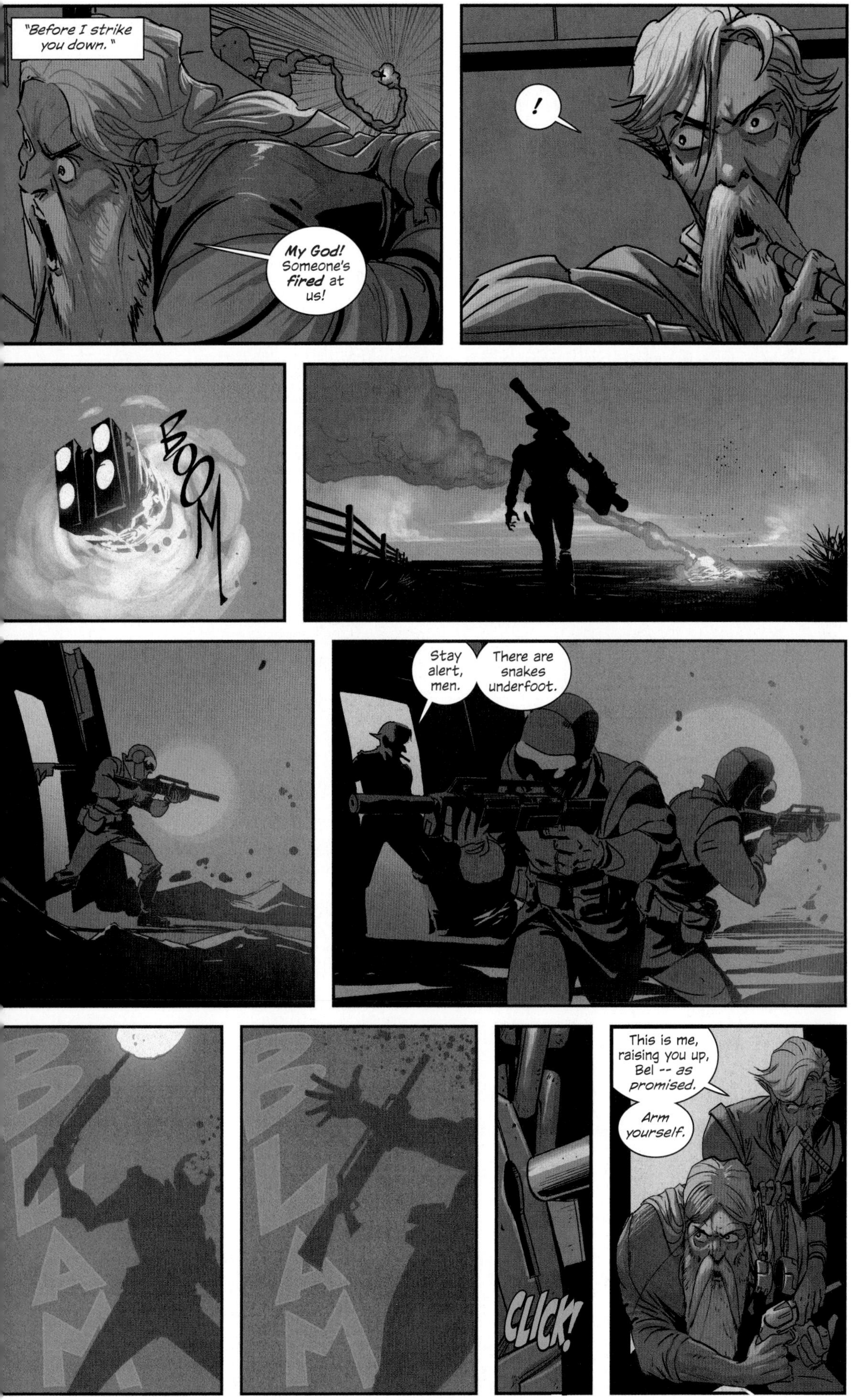
"Before I strike you down."
My God! Someone's fired at us!
!
BOOM
Stay alert, men.
There are snakes underfoot.
BLAM
BLAM
CLICK!
This is me, raising you up, Bel -- as promised.
Arm yourself.

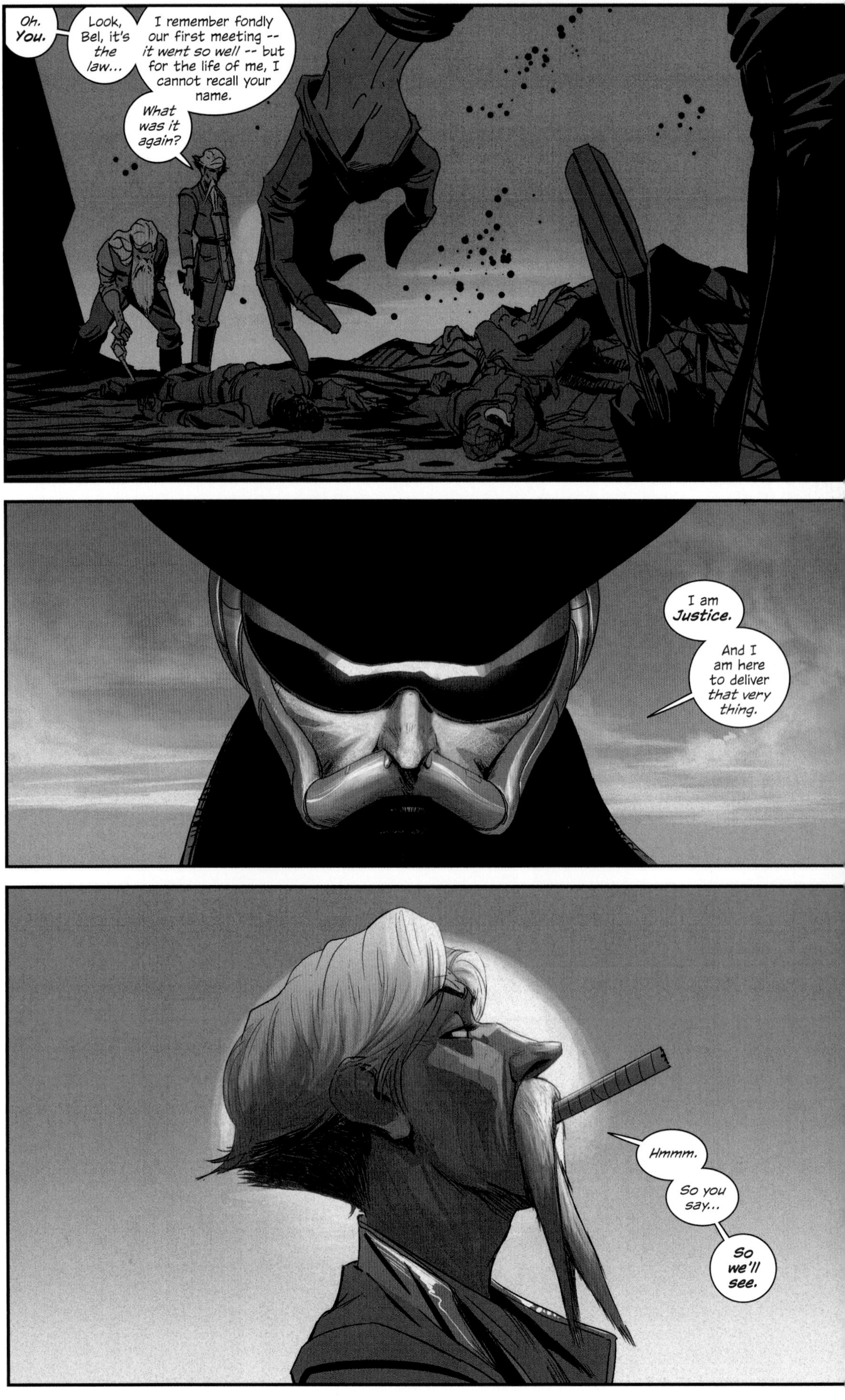
Oh. You.
Look, Bel, it's the law...
I remember fondly our first meeting -- it went so well -- but for the life of me, I cannot recall your name.
What was it again?
I am Justice.
And I am here to deliver that very thing.
Hmmm.
So you say...
So we'll see.

WE **LIVE** LIKE WE WILL
NEVER DIE.

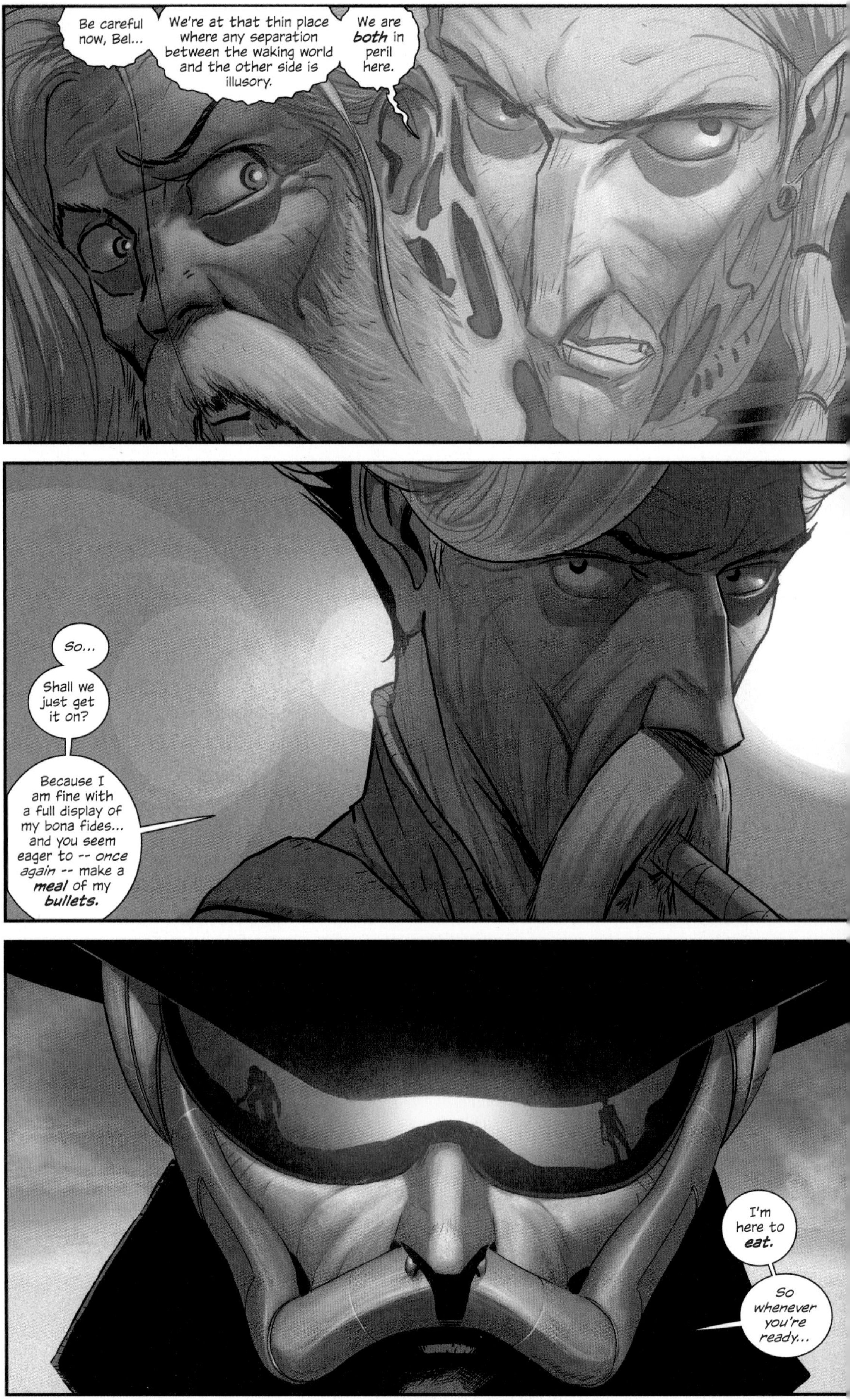

Be careful now, Bel...
We're at that thin place where any separation between the waking world and the other side is illusory.
We are **both** in peril here.
So...
Shall we just get it on?
Because I am fine with a full display of my bona fides... and you seem eager to -- *once again* -- make a ***meal*** of my ***bullets.***
I'm here to ***eat.***
So whenever you're ready...

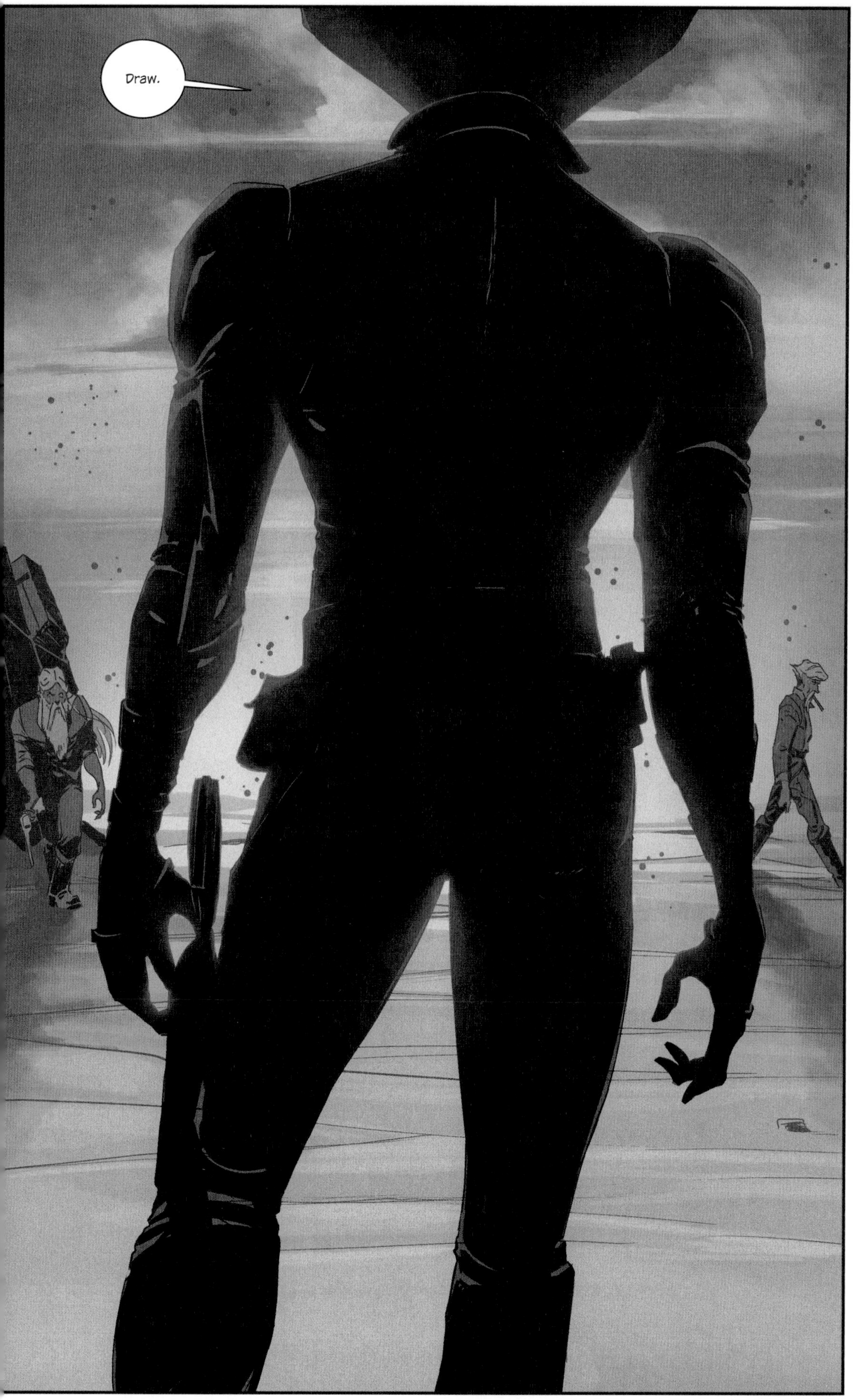
Draw.

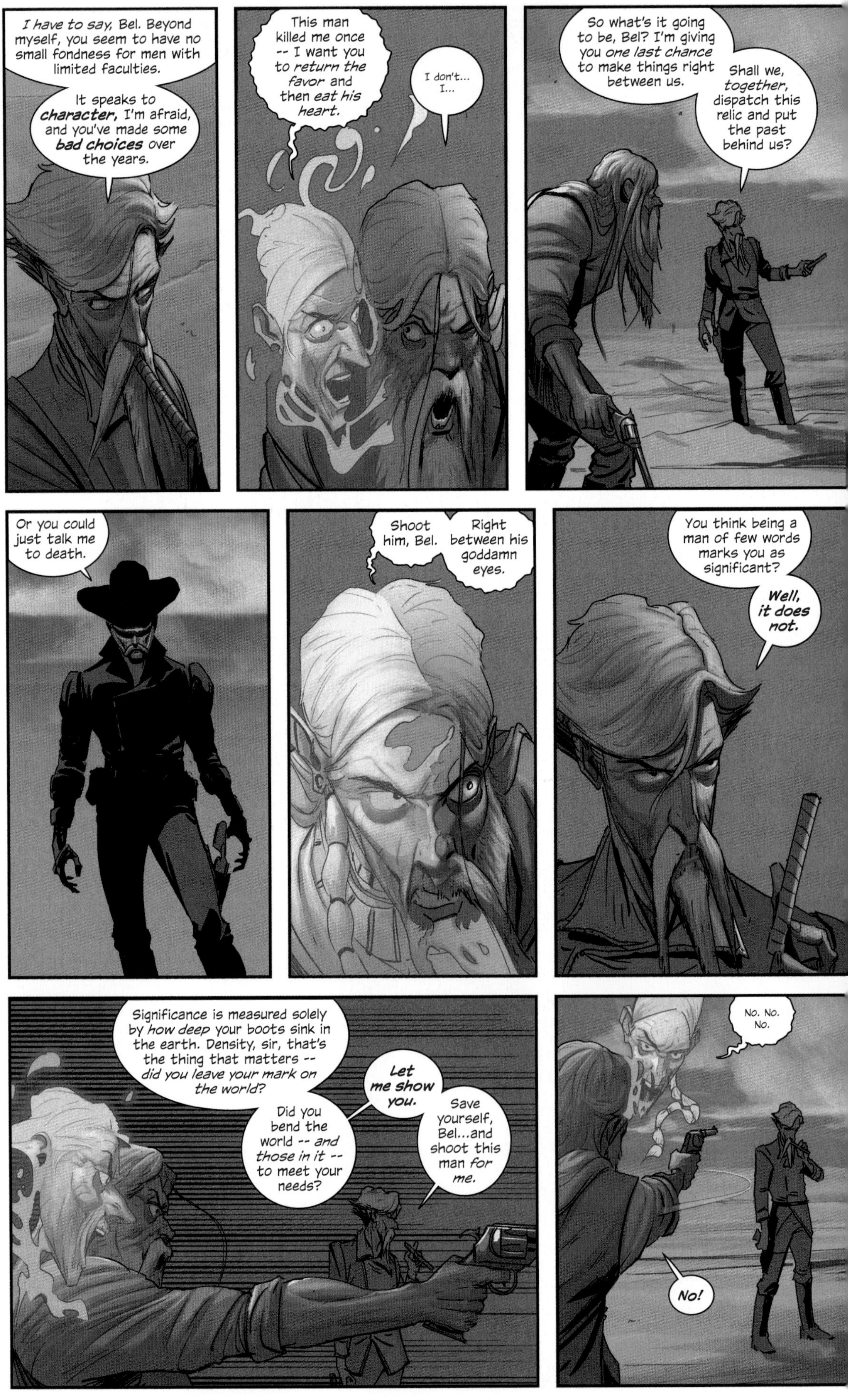
I have to say, Bel. Beyond myself, you seem to have no small fondness for men with limited faculties.
It speaks to character, I'm afraid, and you've made some bad choices over the years.
This man killed me once -- I want you to return the favor and then eat his heart.
I don't... I...
So what's it going to be, Bel? I'm giving you one last chance to make things right between us.
Shall we, together, dispatch this relic and put the past behind us?
Or you could just talk me to death.
Shoot him, Bel.
Right between his goddamn eyes.
You think being a man of few words marks you as significant?
Well, it does not.
Significance is measured solely by how deep your boots sink in the earth. Density, sir, that's the thing that matters -- did you leave your mark on the world?
Did you bend the world -- and those in it -- to meet your needs?
Let me show you.
Save yourself, Bel...and shoot this man for me.
No. No. No.
No!

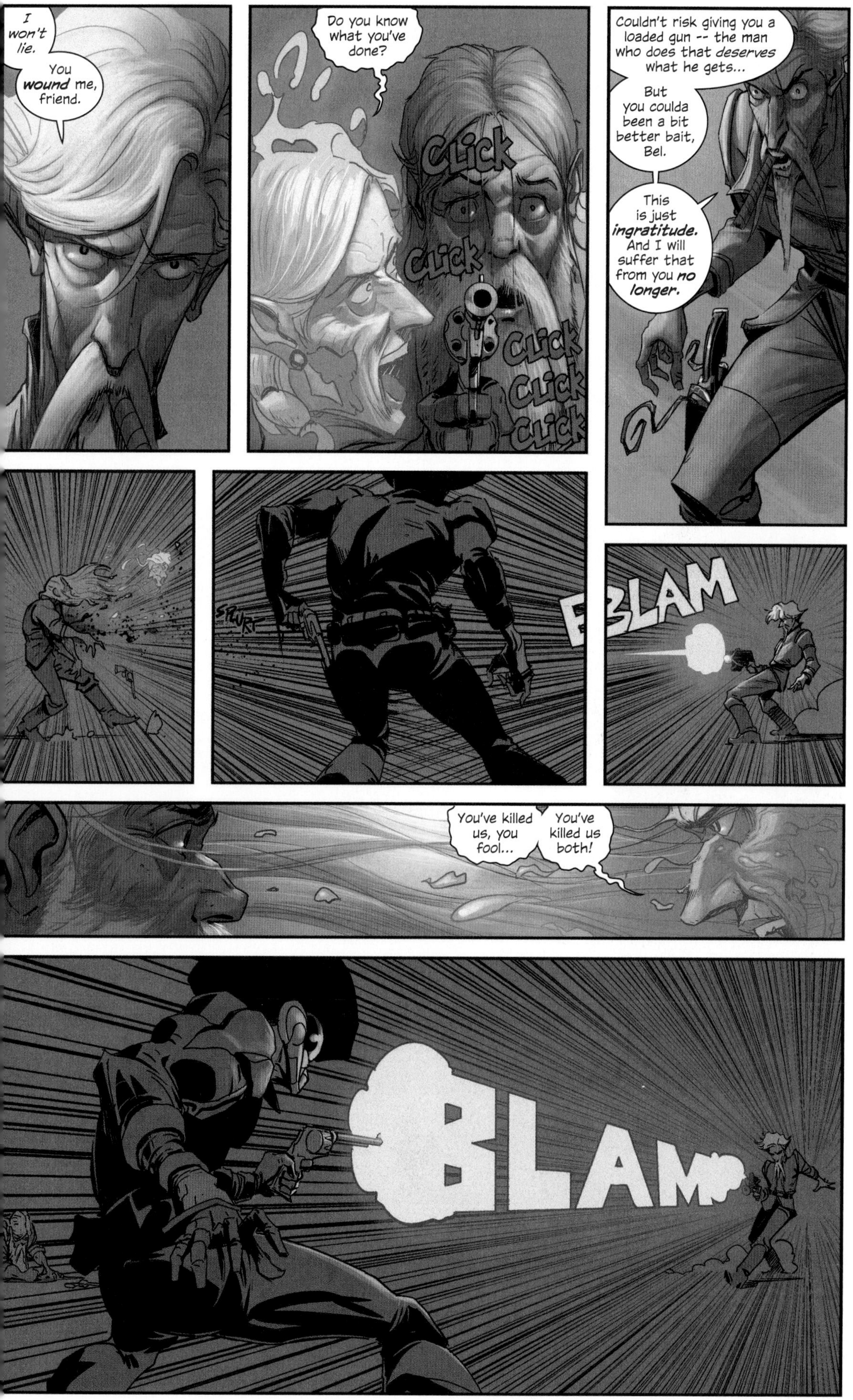
I won't lie.
You *wound* me, friend.
Do you know what you've done?
CLICK
CLICK
CLICK
CLICK
CLICK
Couldn't risk giving you a loaded gun -- the man who does that *deserves* what he gets...
But you coulda been a bit better bait, Bel.
This is just *ingratitude.* And I will suffer that from you *no longer.*
BLAM
You've killed us, you fool...
You've killed us both!
BLAM

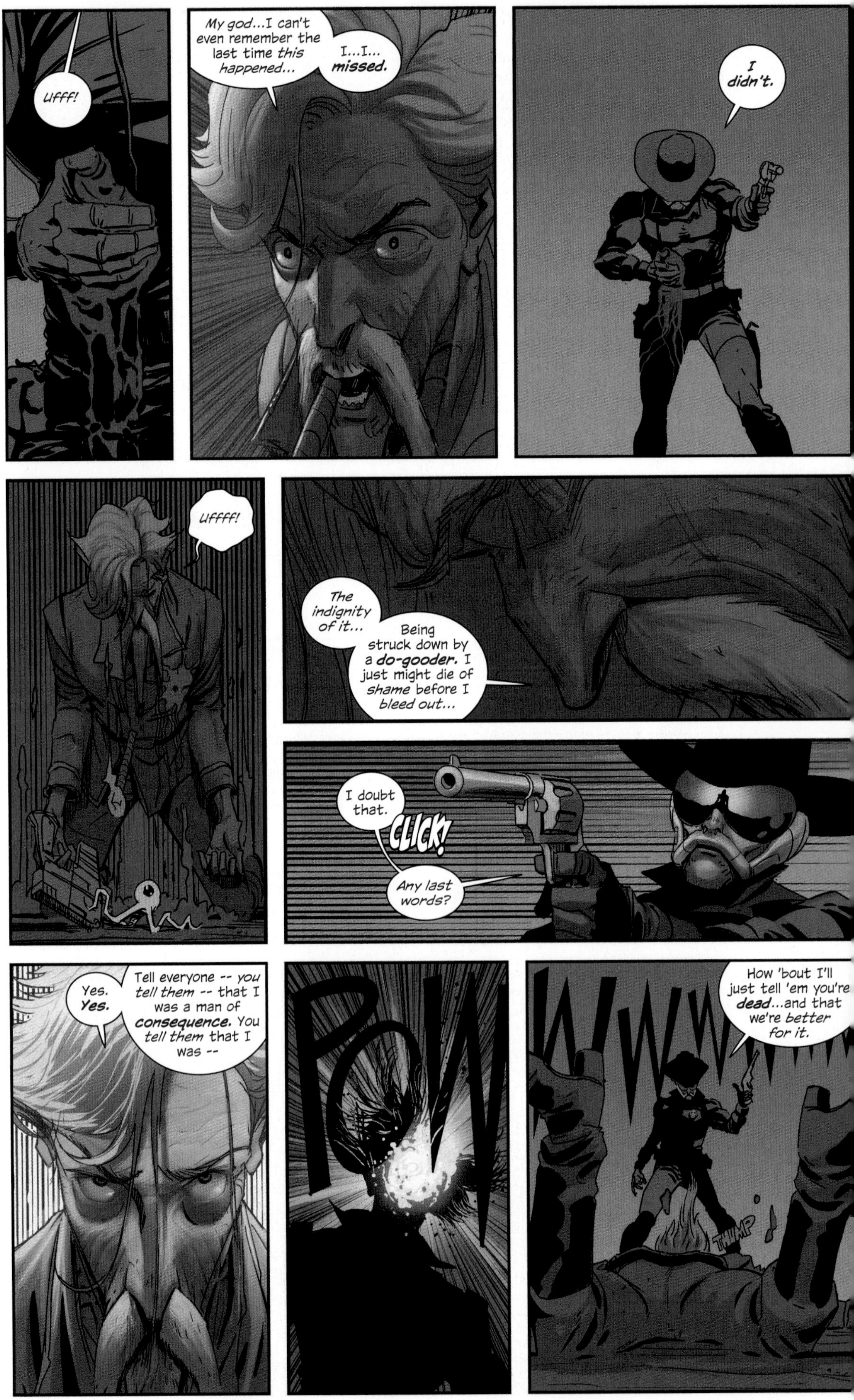
Ufff!
My god...I can't even remember the last time this happened...
I...I... missed.
I didn't.
Uffff!
The indignity of it...
Being struck down by a do-gooder. I just might die of shame before I bleed out...
I doubt that.
CLICK!
Any last words?
Yes. Yes.
Tell everyone -- you tell them -- that I was a man of consequence. You tell them that I was --
POW
How 'bout I'll just tell 'em you're dead...and that we're better for it.
THUMP

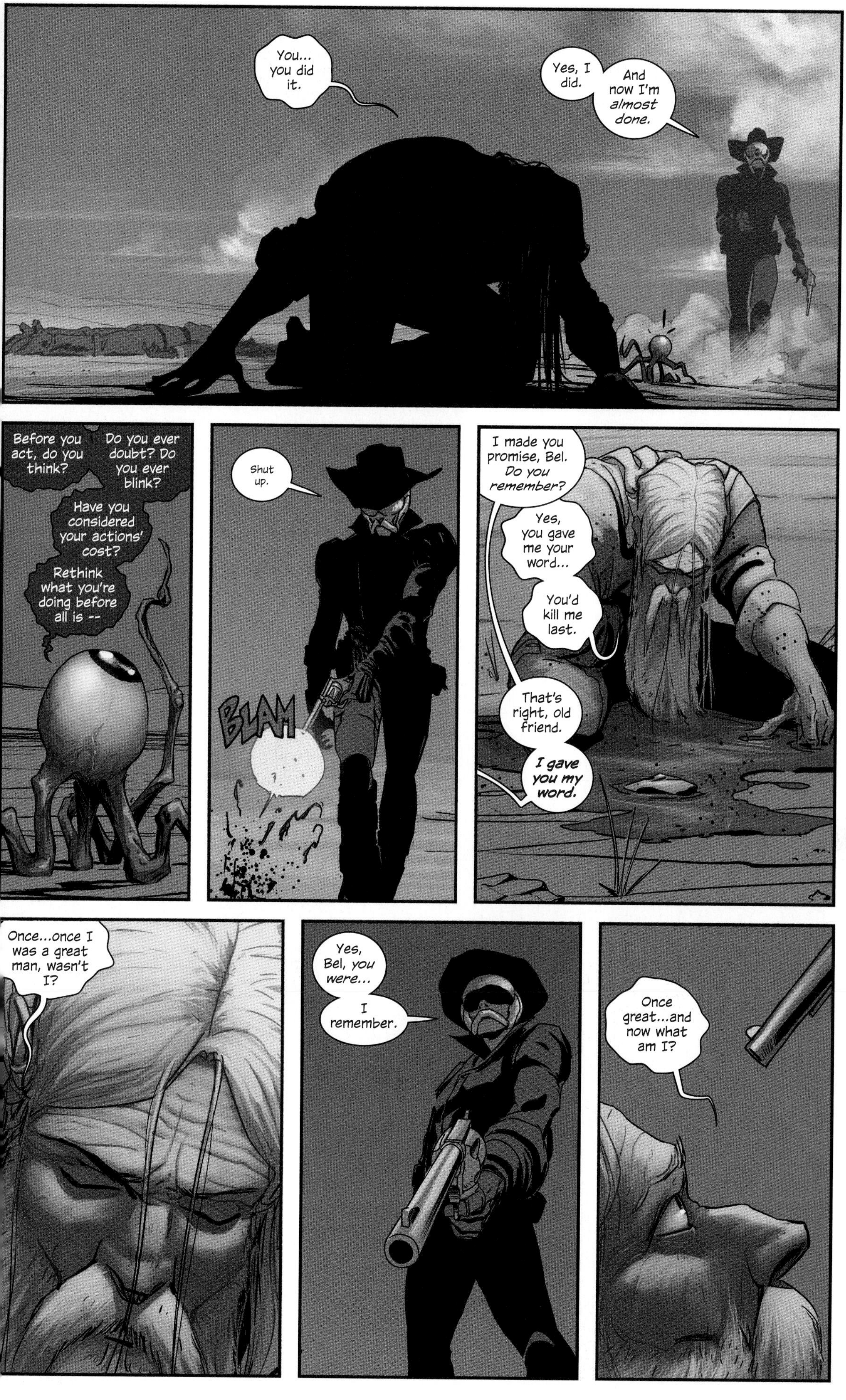
You... you did it.
Yes, I did.
And now I'm *almost* done.
Before you act, do you think?
Do you ever doubt? Do you ever blink?
Have you considered your actions' cost?
Rethink what you're doing before all is --
Shut up.
BLAM
I made you promise, Bel. *Do you remember?*
Yes, you gave me your word...
You'd kill me last.
That's right, old friend.
I gave you my word.
Once...once I was a great man, wasn't I?
Yes, Bel, *you were...*
I remember.
Once great...and now what am I?

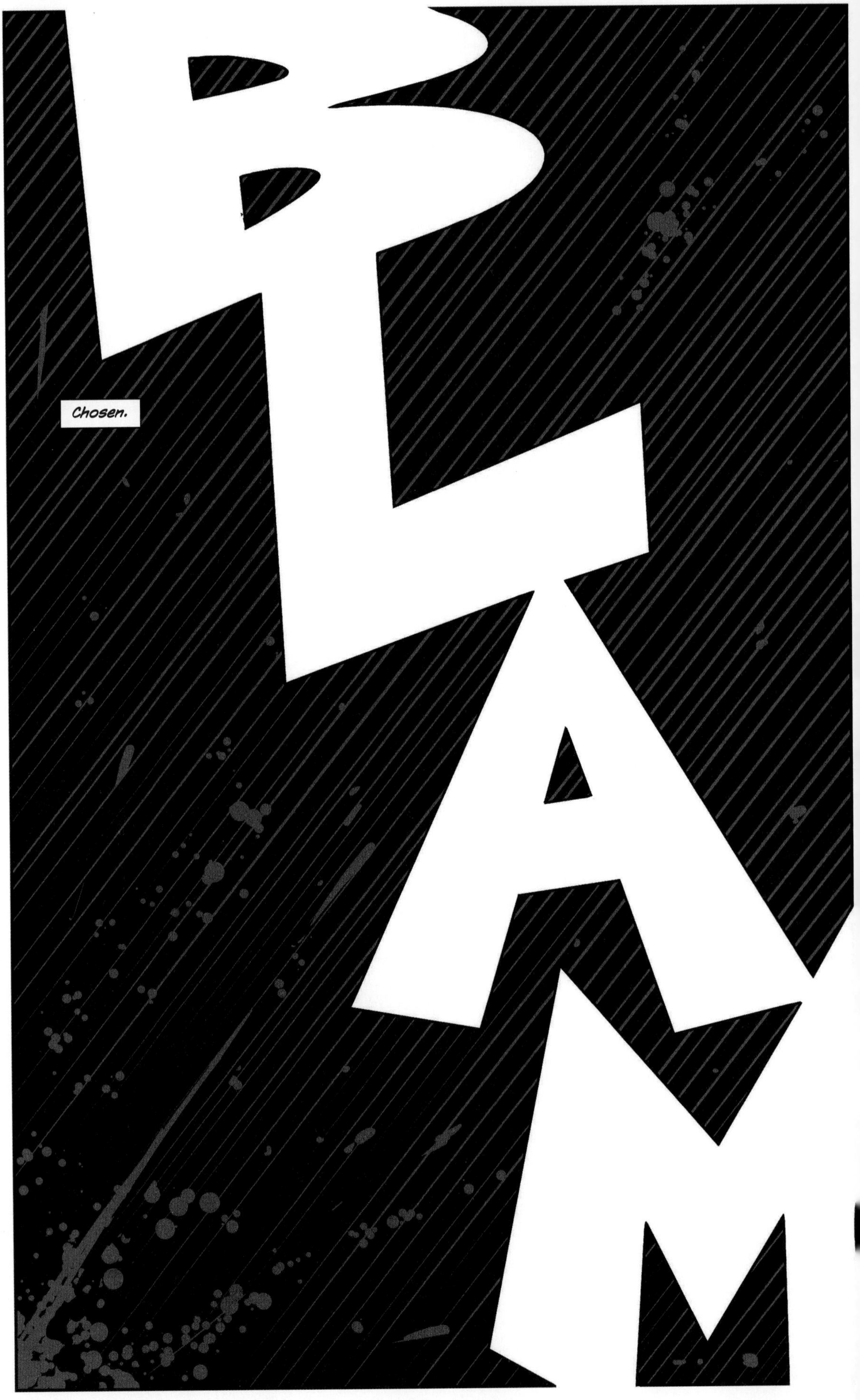
Chosen.
BLAM

WE **DIE** EXACTLY LIKE
WE **LIVED.**

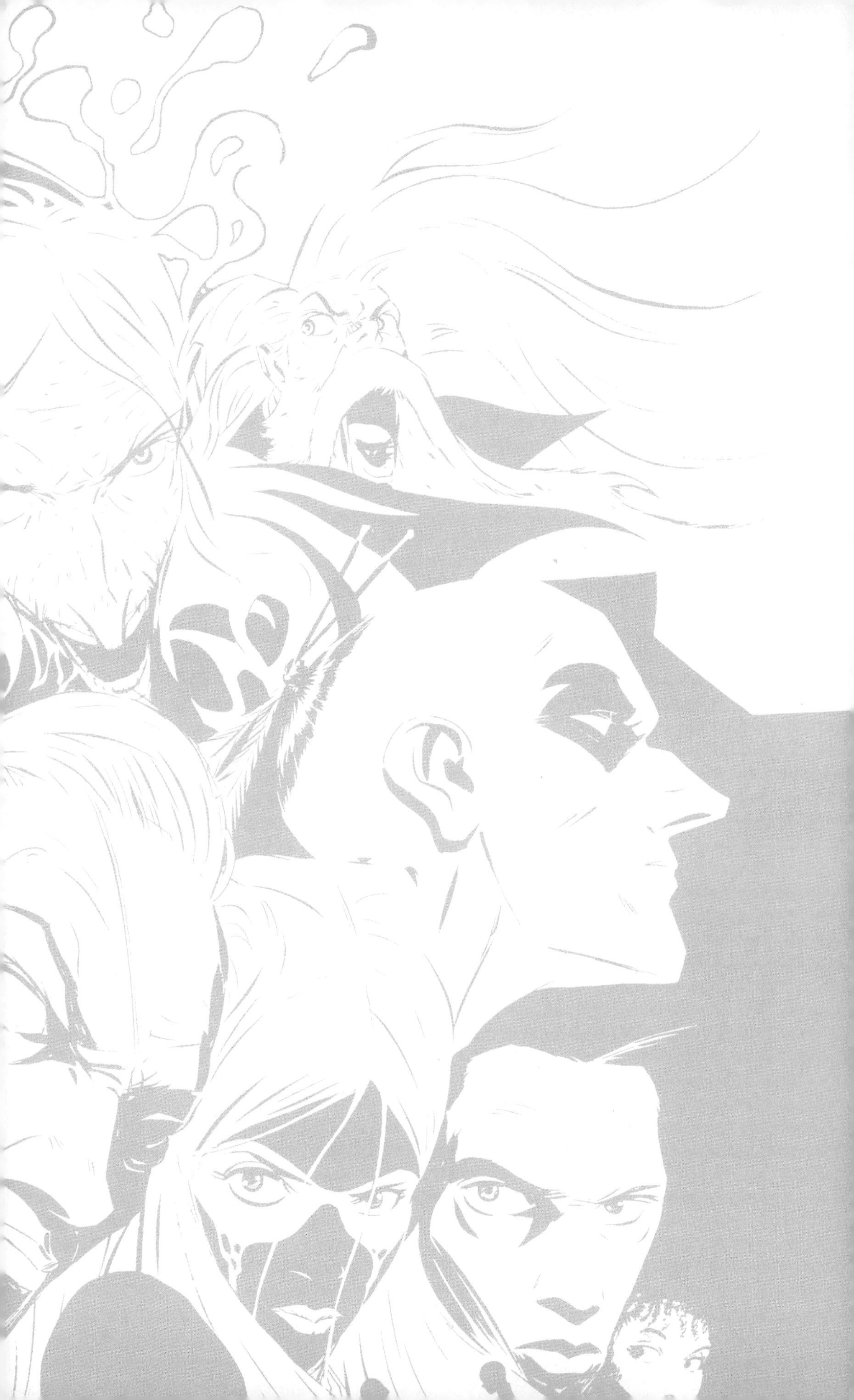

45

**FORTY-FIVE:
APOCALYPSE**

IT HAS **ALWAYS** BEEN **THIS WAY.**

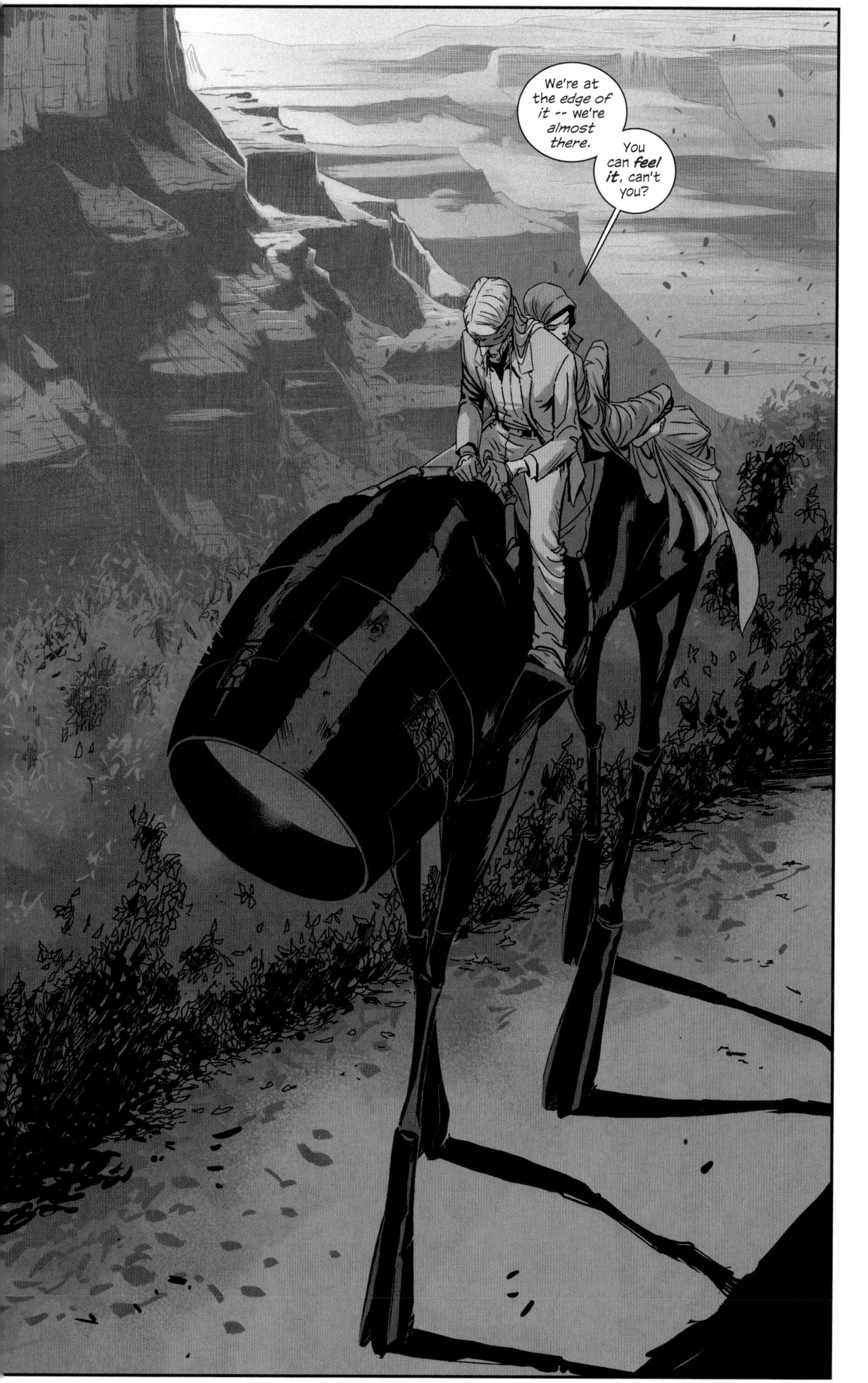
We're at the *edge of it* -- we're *almost there.*
You can ***feel it***, can't you?

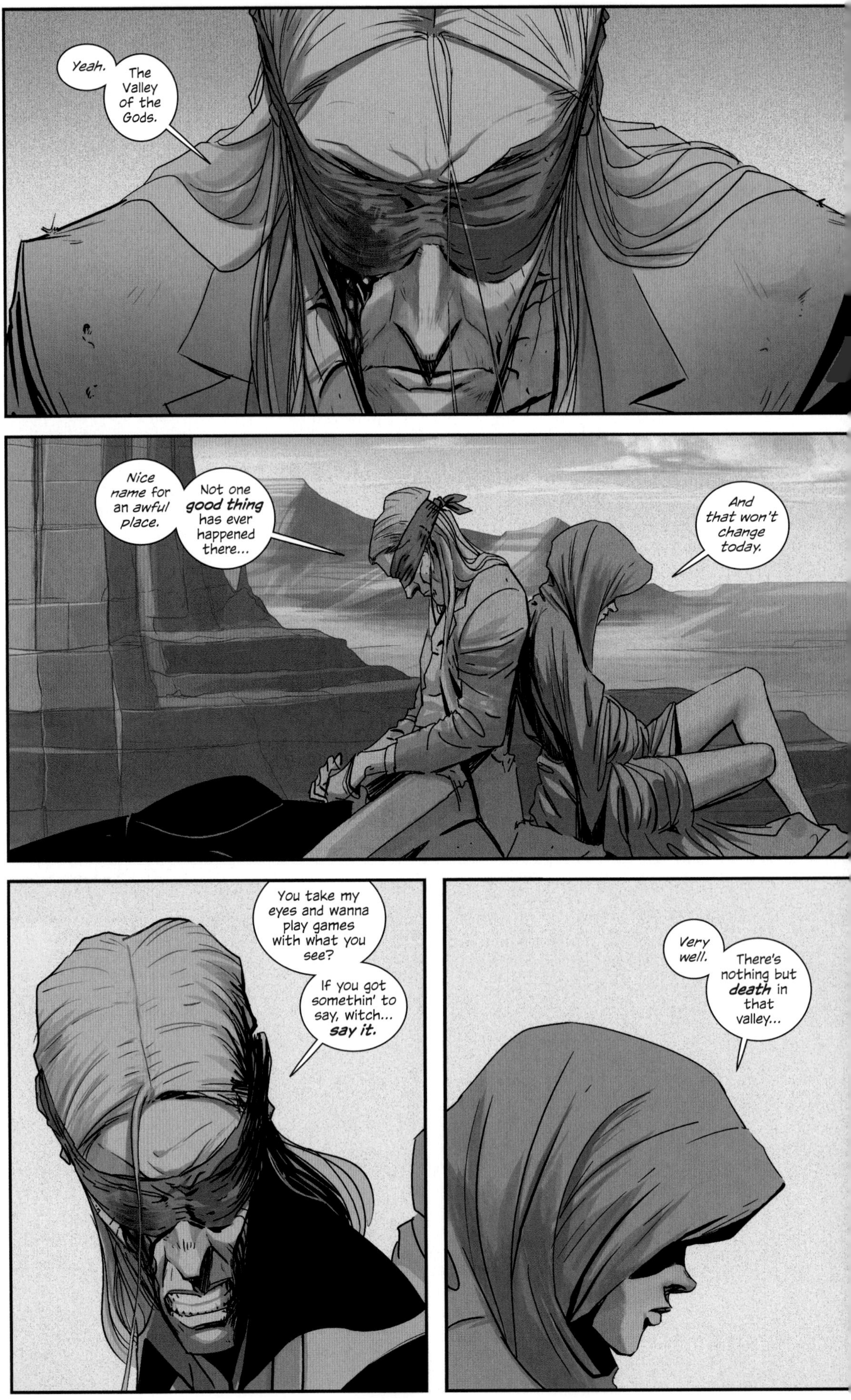
Yeah.
The Valley of the Gods.
Nice name for an awful place.
Not one good thing has ever happened there...
And that won't change today.
You take my eyes and wanna play games with what you see?
If you got somethin' to say, witch... say it.
Very well.
There's nothing but death in that valley...

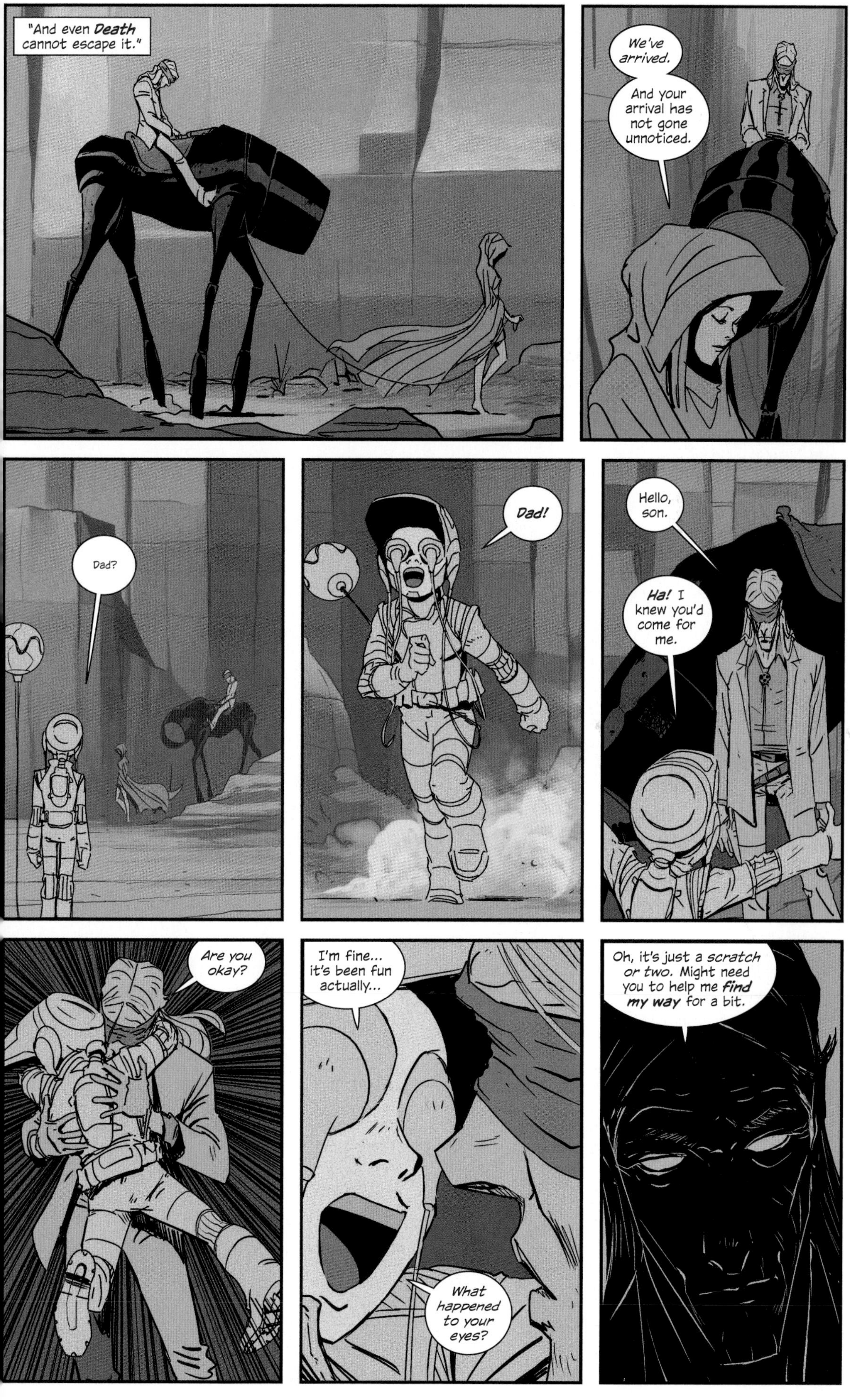
"And even *Death* cannot escape it."
We've arrived.
And your arrival has not gone unnoticed.
Dad?
Dad!
Hello, son.
Ha! I knew you'd come for me.
Are you okay?
I'm fine... it's been fun actually...
What happened to your eyes?
Oh, it's just a *scratch or two.* Might need you to help me ***find my way*** for a bit.

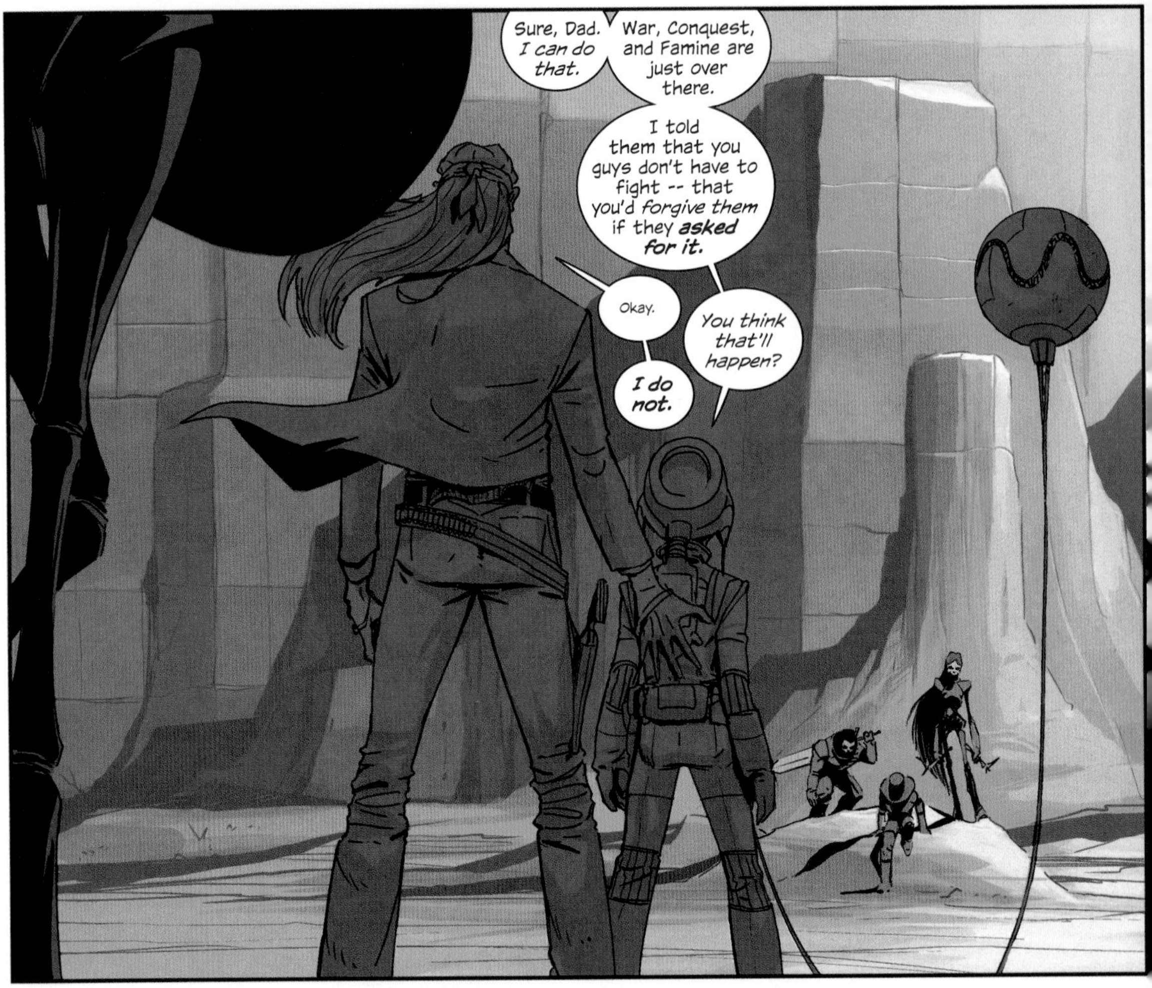
Sure, Dad. I can do that.
War, Conquest, and Famine are just over there.
I told them that you guys don't have to fight -- that you'd forgive them if they asked for it.
Okay.
I do not.
You think that'll happen?

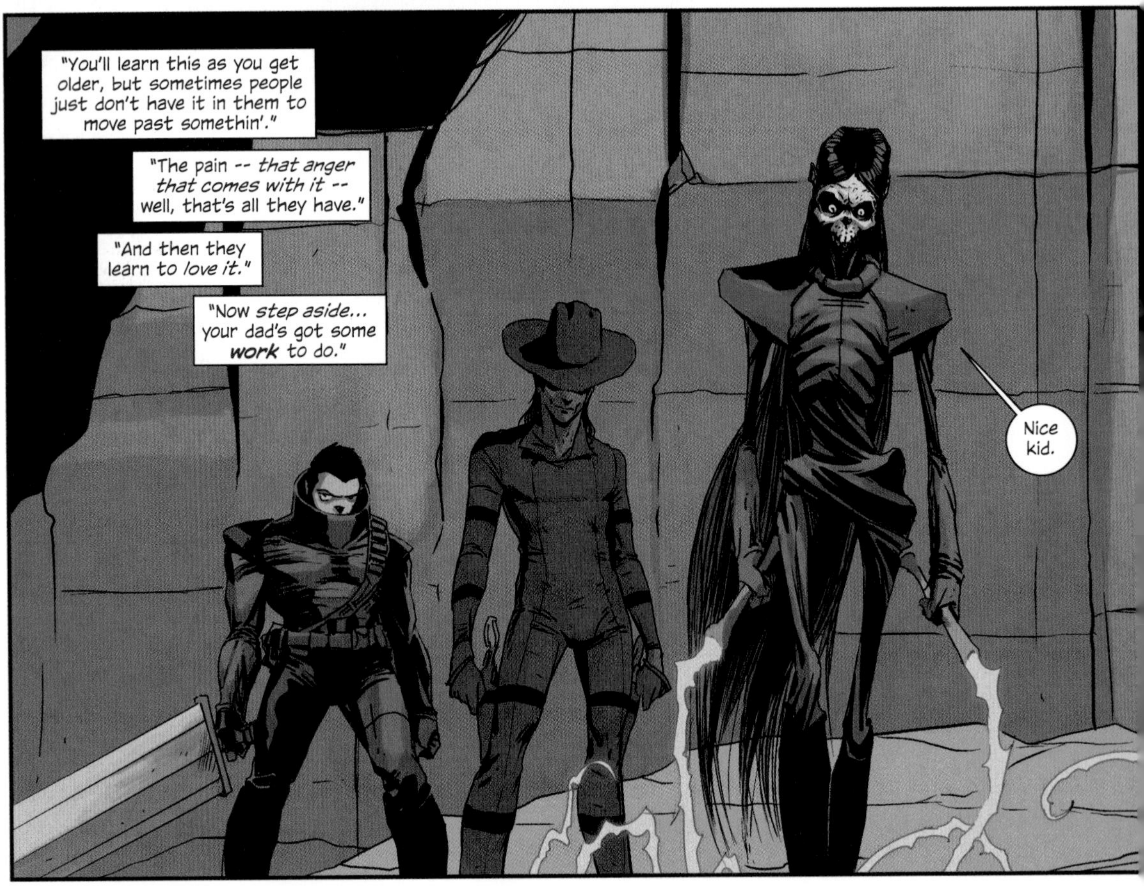
"You'll learn this as you get older, but sometimes people just don't have it in them to move past somethin'."
"The pain -- that anger that comes with it -- well, that's all they have."
"And then they learn to love it."
"Now step aside... your dad's got some work to do."
Nice kid.

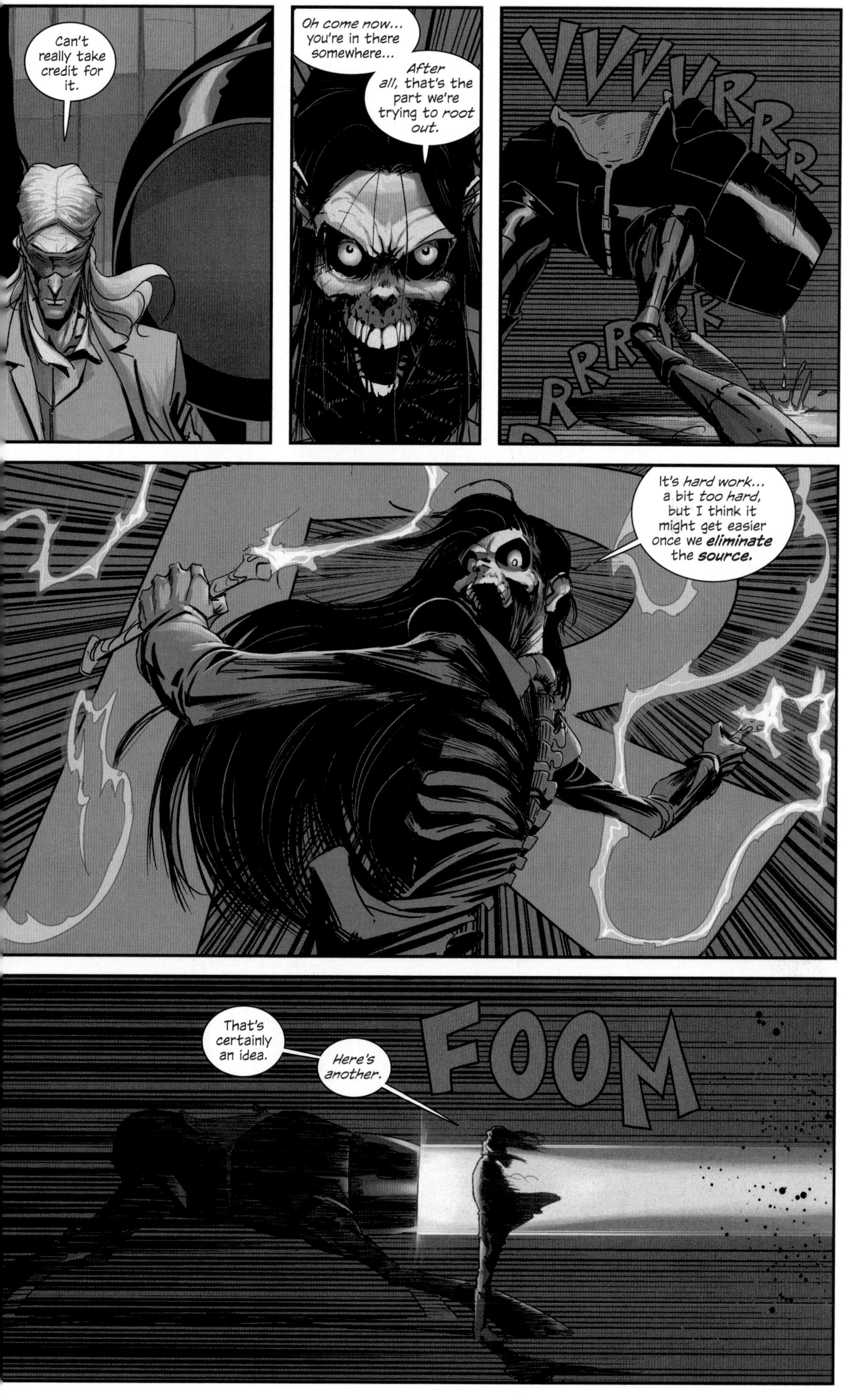

Can't really take credit for it.
Oh come now... you're in there somewhere...
After all, that's the part we're trying to root out.
VVVVRRRR
RRRRRRR
It's hard work... a bit too hard, but I think it might get easier once we eliminate the source.
That's certainly an idea.
Here's another.
FOOM

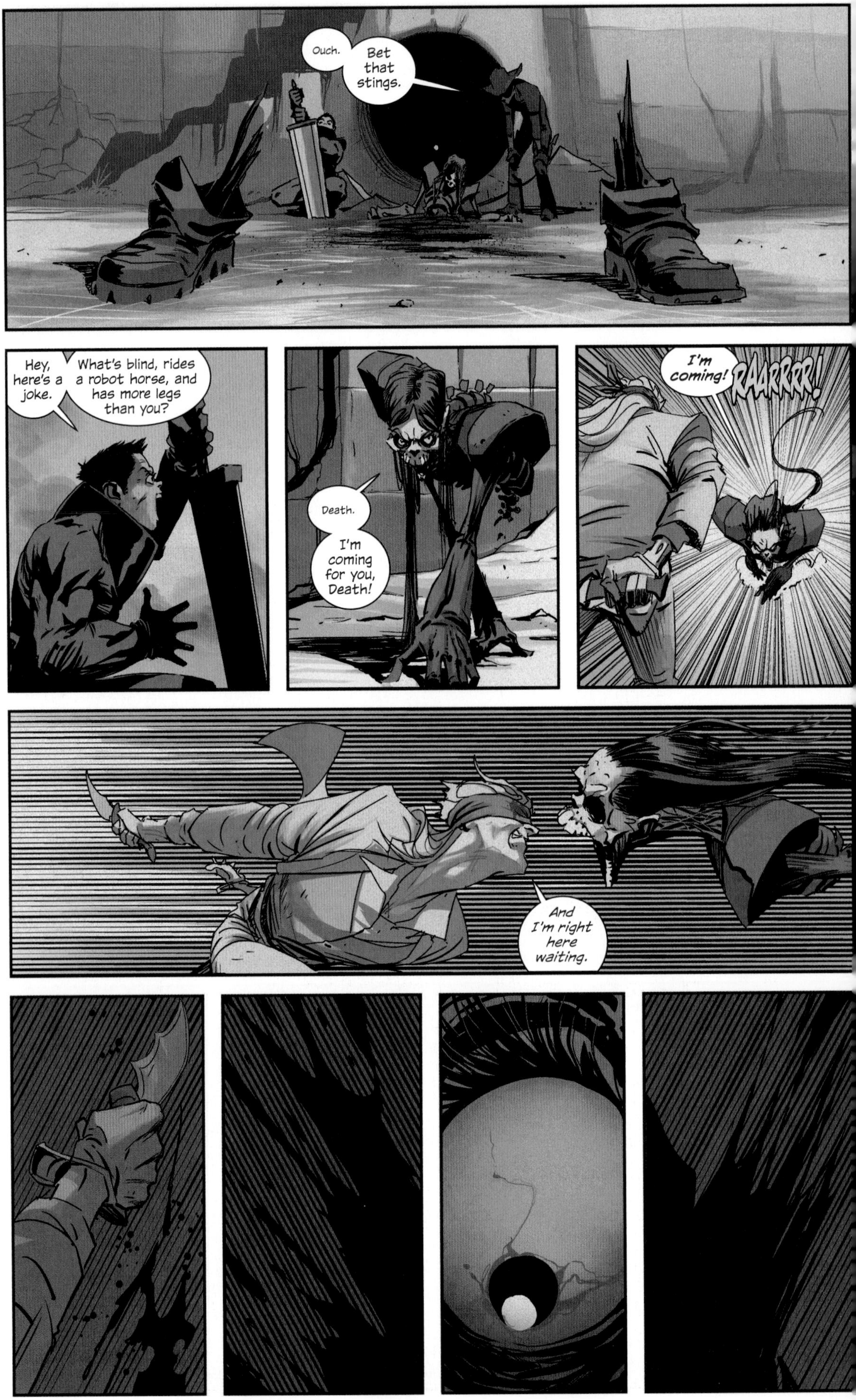
Ouch.
Bet that stings.
Hey, here's a joke.
What's blind, rides a robot horse, and has more legs than you?
Death.
I'm coming for you, Death!
I'm coming!
RAARRRR!
And I'm right here waiting.

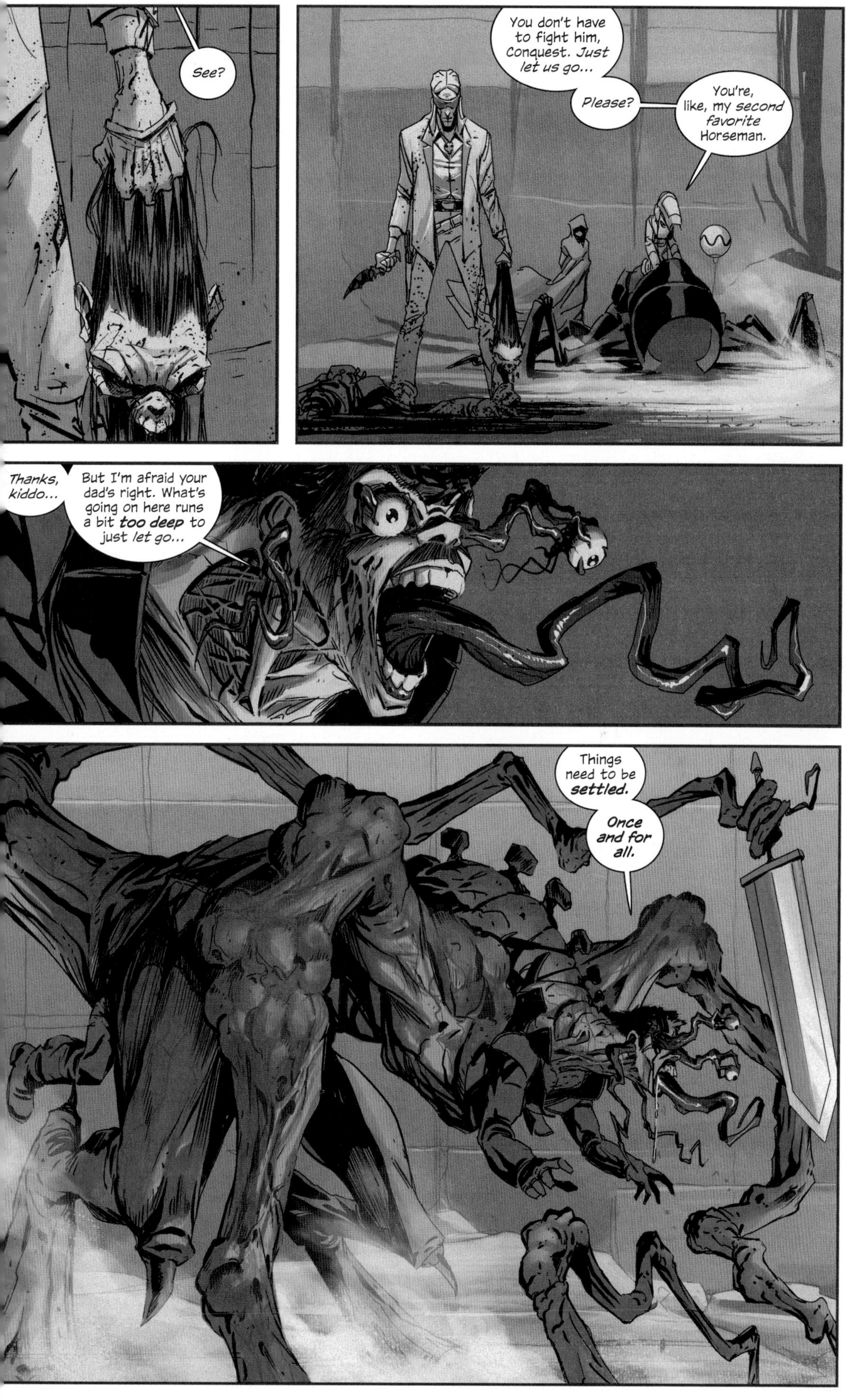
See?
You don't have to fight him, Conquest. Just let us go...
Please?
You're, like, my second favorite Horseman.
Thanks, kiddo...
But I'm afraid your dad's right. What's going on here runs a bit **too deep** to just *let go*...
Things need to be **settled.**
Once and for all.

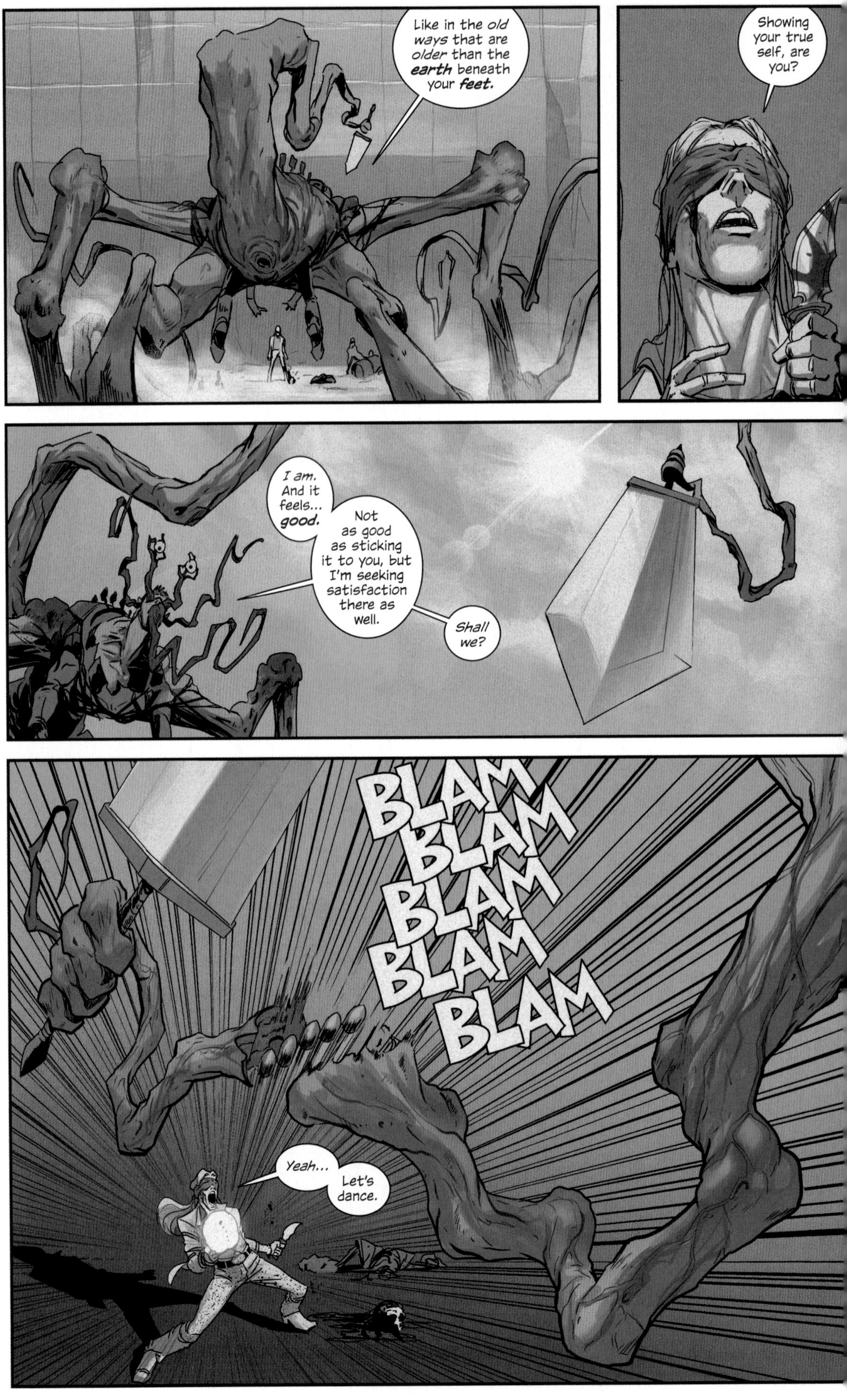
Like in the *old ways* that are *older* than the **earth** beneath your **feet.**
Showing your true self, are you?
I am. And it feels... **good.**
Not as good as sticking it to you, but I'm seeking satisfaction there as well.
Shall we?
BLAM BLAM BLAM BLAM BLAM
Yeah...
Let's dance.

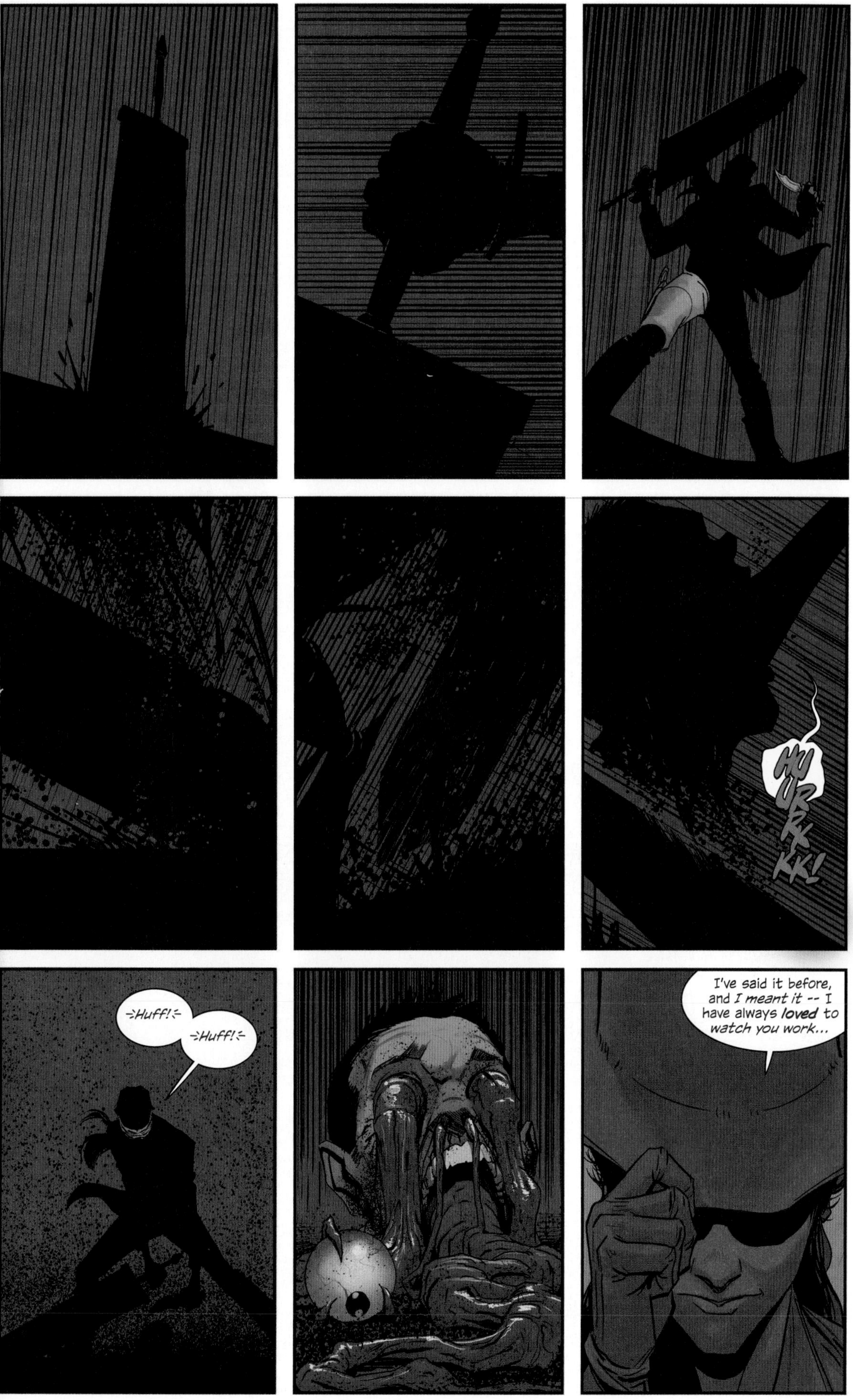
HUURKKK!
Huff!
Huff!
I've said it before, and I meant it -- I have always loved to watch you work...

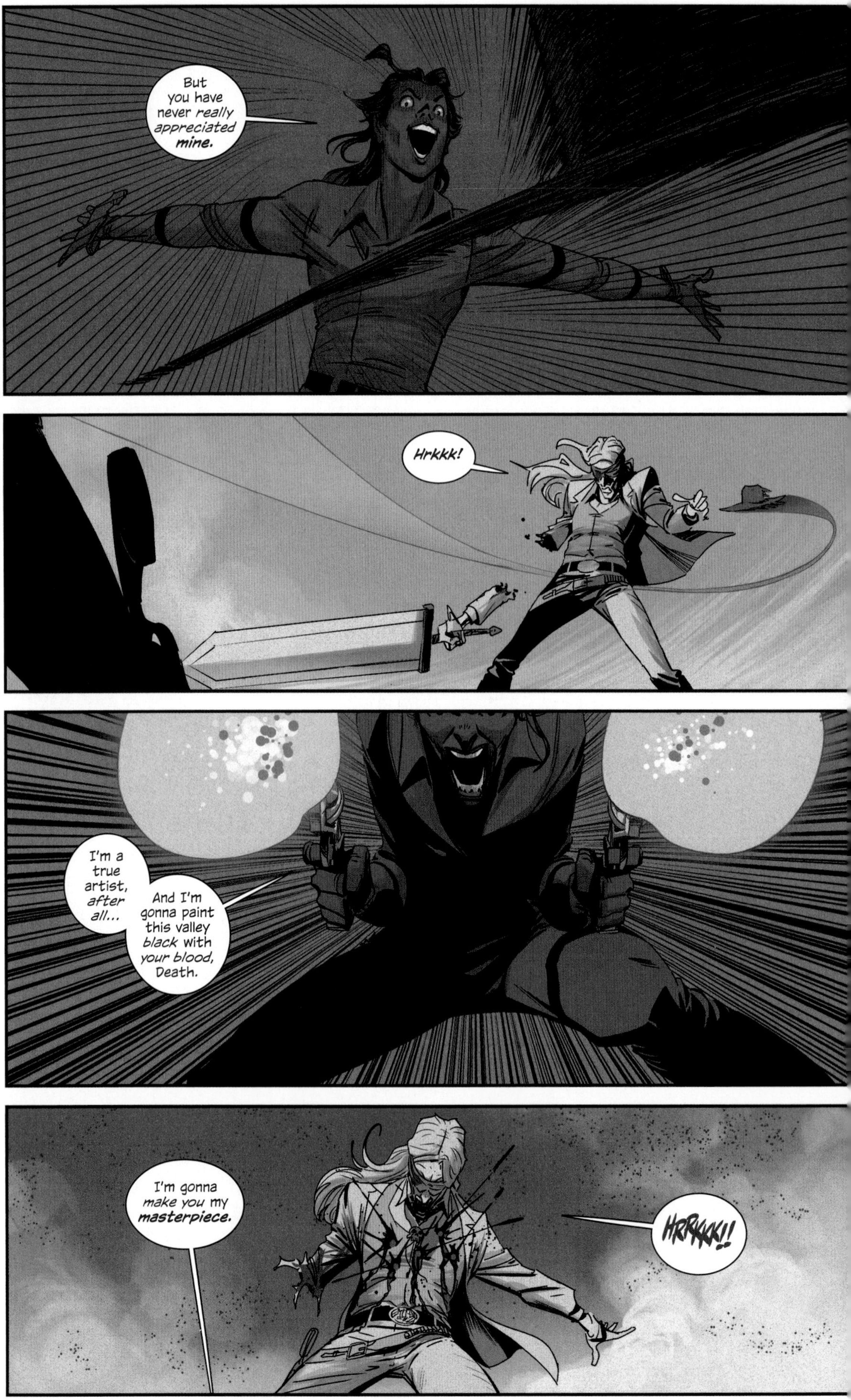
But you have never *really* *appreciated* **mine.**
Hrkkk!
I'm a true artist, *after all...*
And I'm gonna paint this valley *black* with *your blood,* Death.
I'm gonna *make you my* **masterpiece.**
HRRKKK!!

Dad! Balloon, how is--

Severed limb, multiple gunshot wounds, extreme blood loss. He's critical, Babylon.

Dad! **Dad!** You have to get up!

When I'm done with him, boy -- I'm making a meal out of you.

Babylon... move away from me. *Move!*

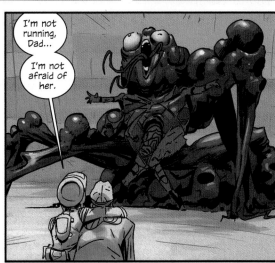

I'm not running, Dad... I'm not afraid of her.

Not afraid? *Ha!* In the end, you will be.

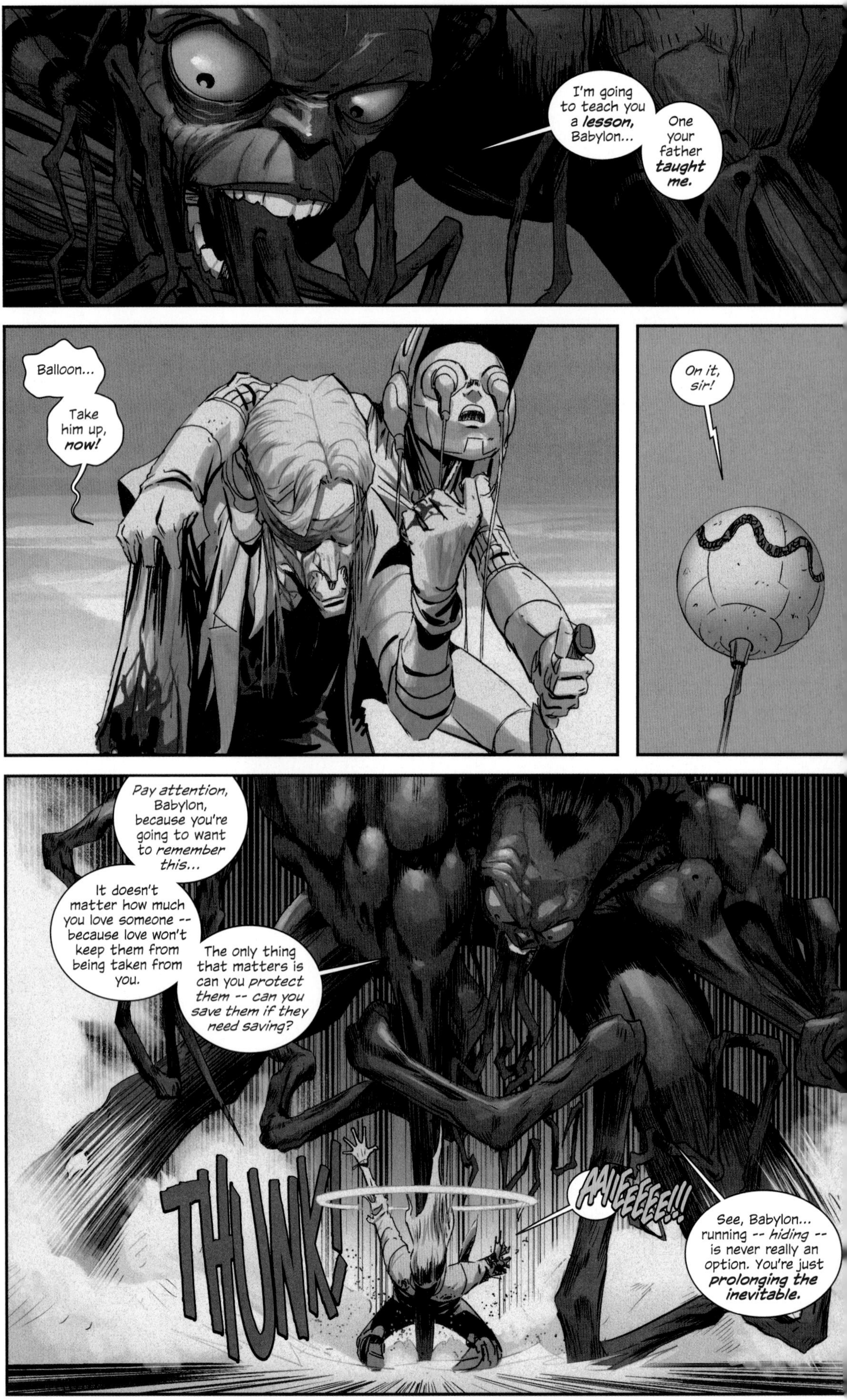

I'm going to teach you a *lesson,* Babylon...
One your father ***taught me.***
Balloon...
Take him up, ***now!***
On it, sir!
Pay attention, Babylon, because you're going to want to *remember this...*
It doesn't matter how much you love someone -- because love won't keep them from being taken from you.
The only thing that matters is can you *protect them -- can you save them if they need saving?*
THUNK!
AAIEEEEE!!!
See, Babylon... running -- *hiding* -- is never really an option. You're just ***prolonging the inevitable.***

Who said anything about runnin'?

PEW

Huh?

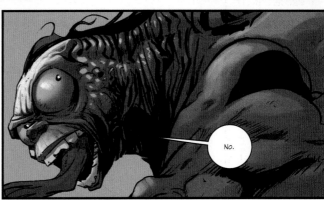

No.

YYAARRR!

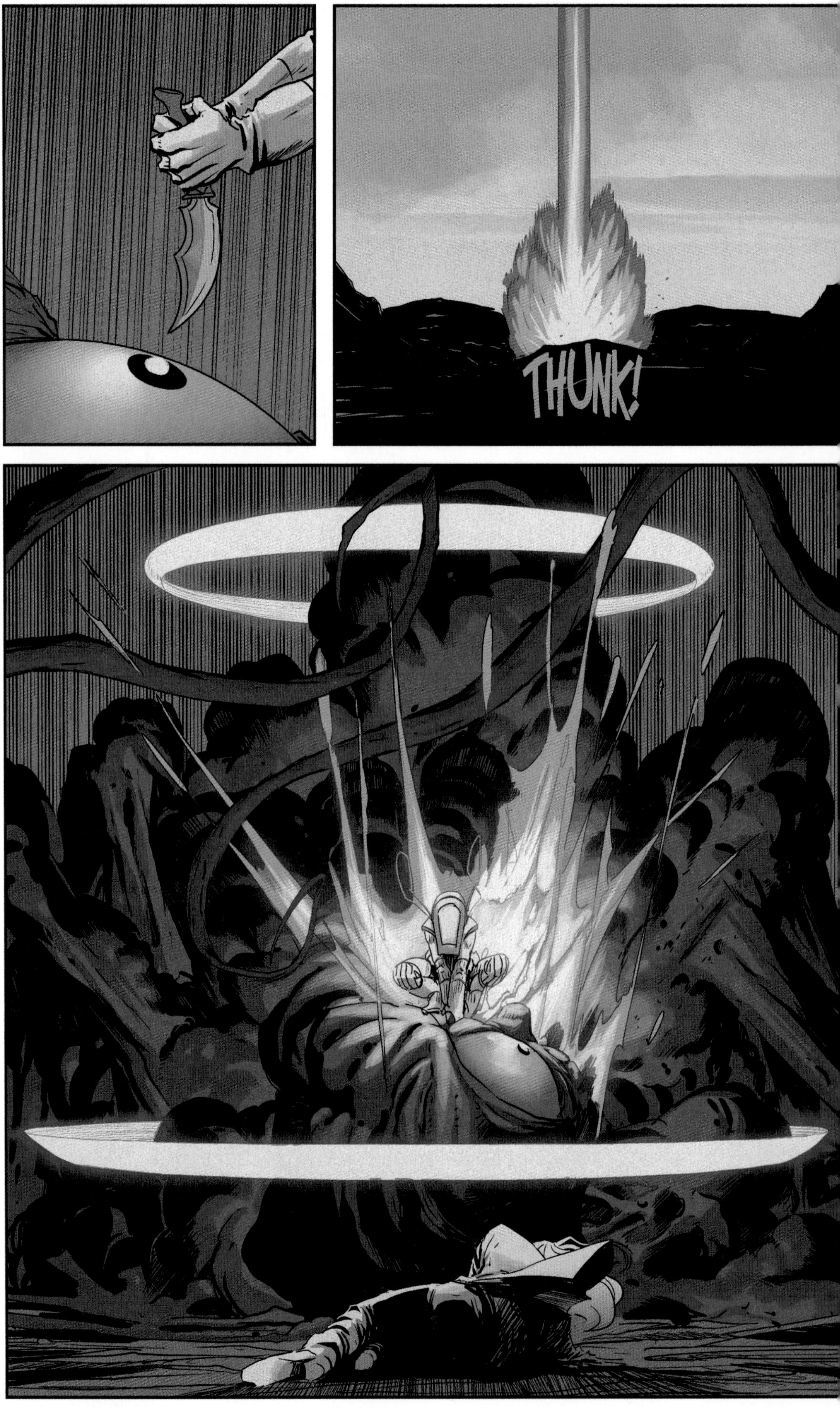
THUNK!

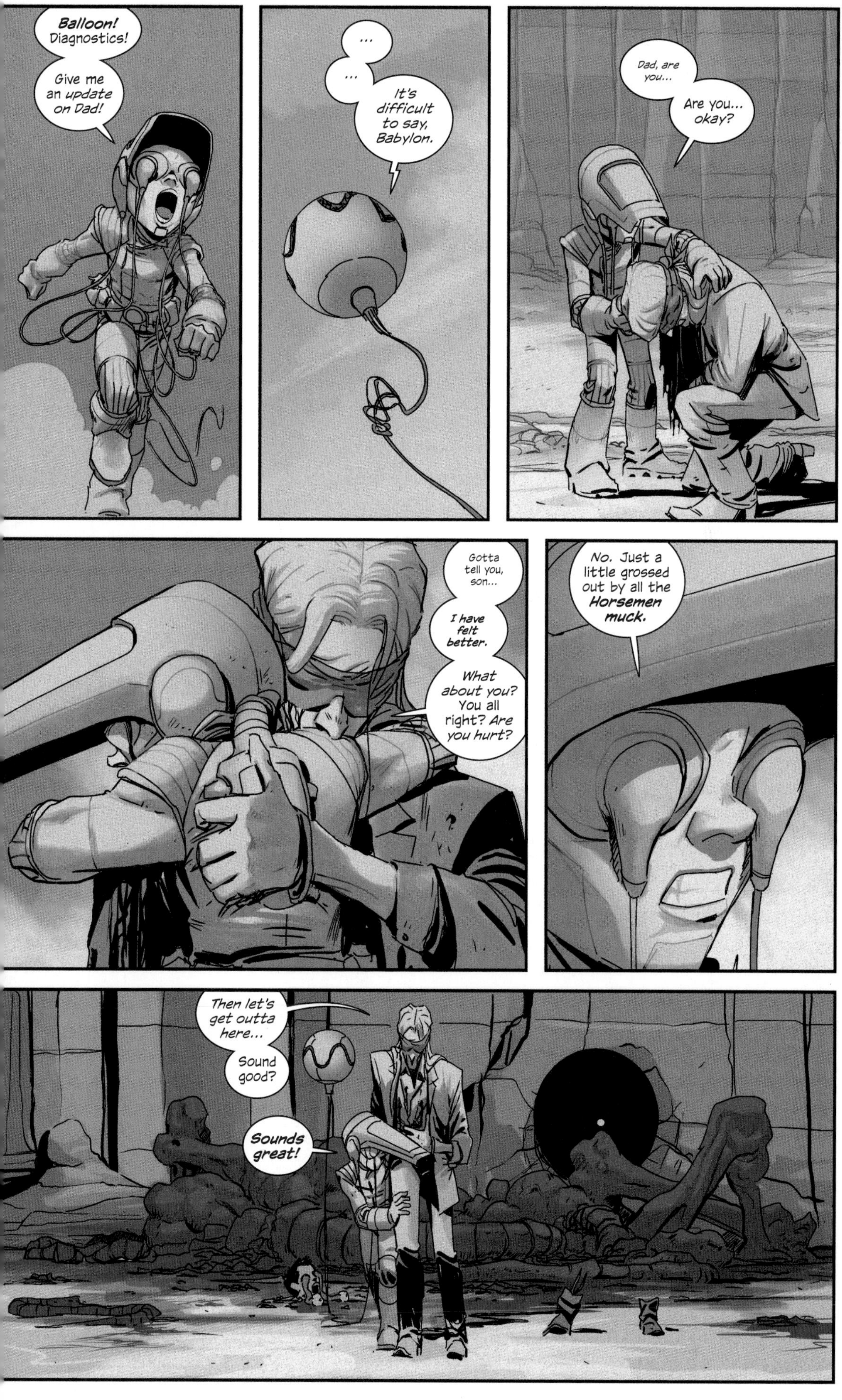
Balloon! Diagnostics!
Give me an update on Dad!
...
...
It's difficult to say, Babylon.
Dad, are you...
Are you... okay?
Gotta tell you, son...
I have felt better.
What about you? You all right? Are you hurt?
No. Just a little grossed out by all the Horsemen muck.
Then let's get outta here...
Sound good?
Sounds great!

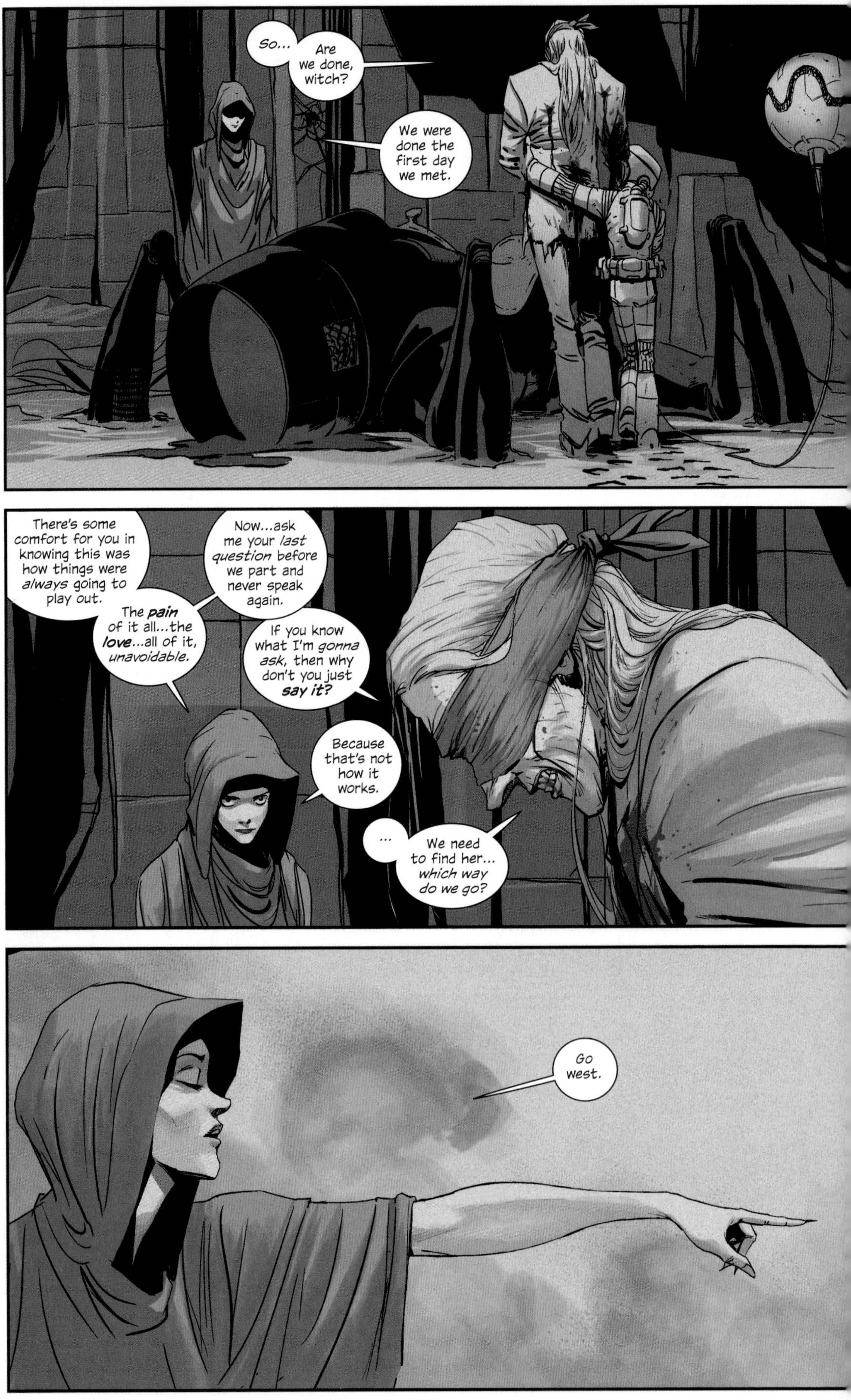
So...
Are we done, witch?
We were done the first day we met.
There's some comfort for you in knowing this was how things were always going to play out.
The pain of it all...the love...all of it, unavoidable.
Now...ask me your last question before we part and never speak again.
If you know what I'm gonna ask, then why don't you just say it?
Because that's not how it works.
...
We need to find her... which way do we go?
Go west.

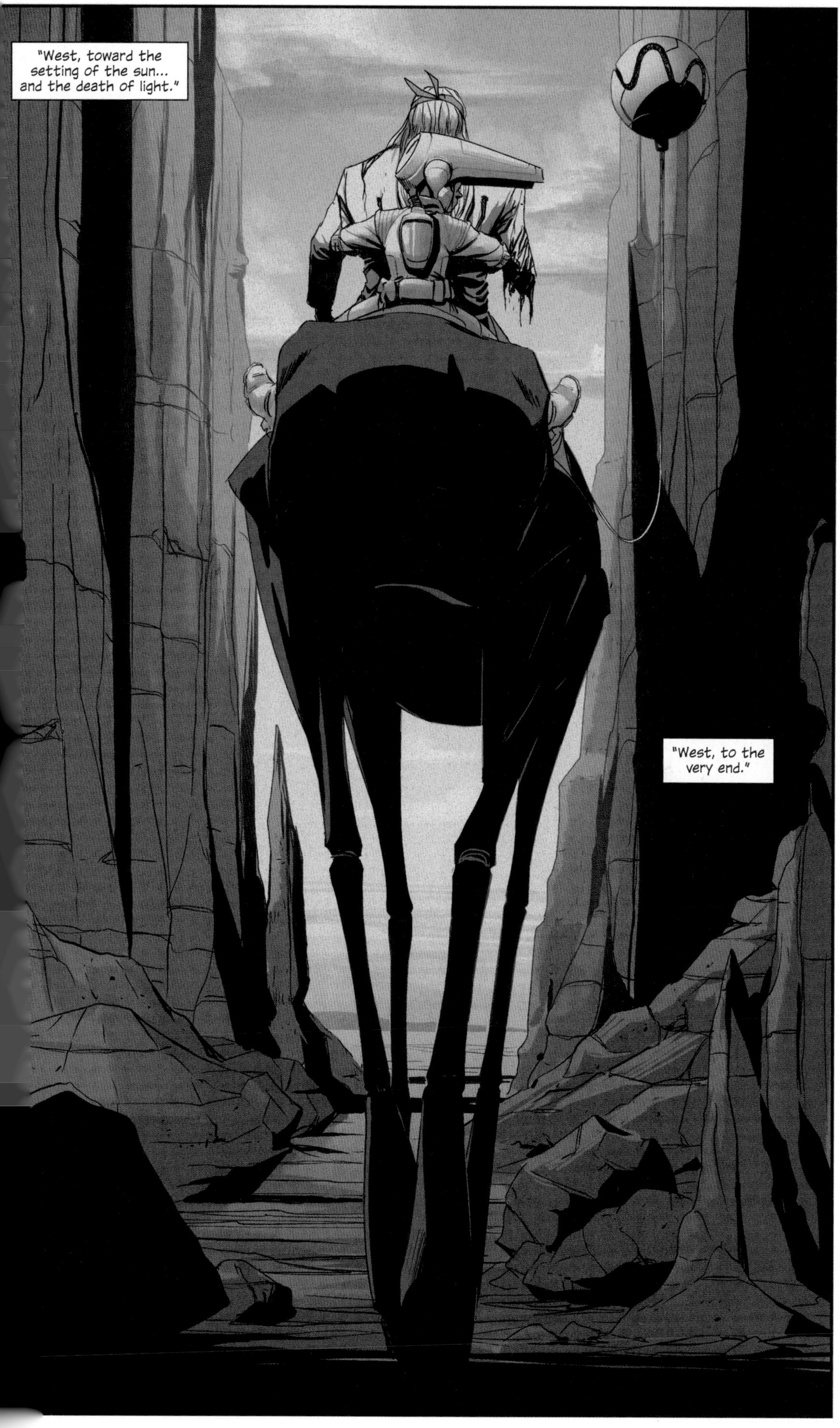
"West, toward the setting of the sun... and the death of light."
"West, to the very end."

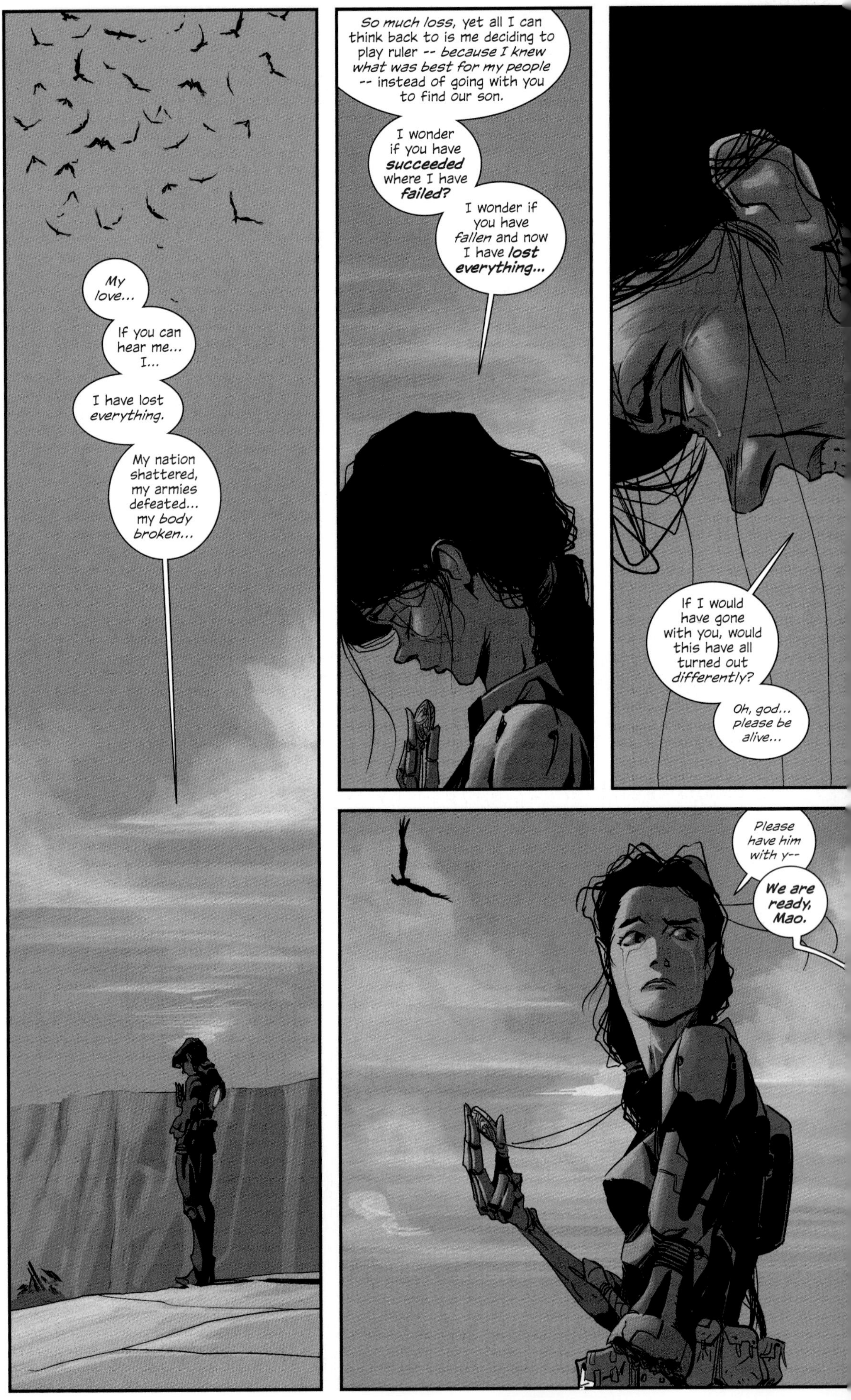
My love...
If you can hear me... I...
I have lost everything.
My nation shattered, my armies defeated... my body broken...
So much loss, yet all I can think back to is me deciding to play ruler -- because I knew what was best for my people -- instead of going with you to find our son.
I wonder if you have succeeded where I have failed?
I wonder if you have fallen and now I have lost everything...
If I would have gone with you, would this have all turned out differently?
Oh, god... please be alive...
Please have him with y--
We are ready, Mao.

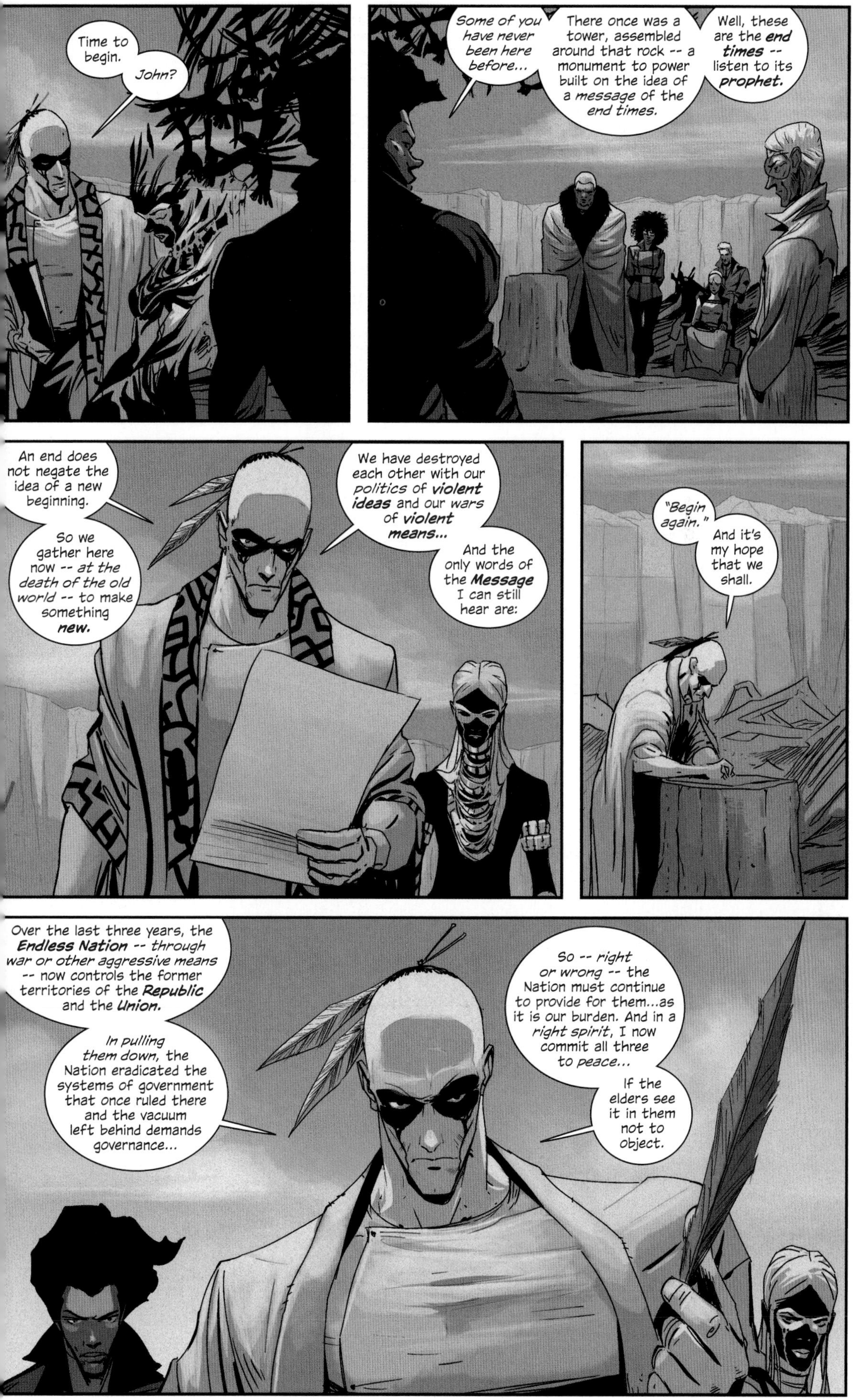

Time to begin.
John?
Some of you have never been here before...
There once was a tower, assembled around that rock -- a monument to power built on the idea of a message of the end times.
Well, these are the end times -- listen to its prophet.
An end does not negate the idea of a new beginning.
So we gather here now -- at the death of the old world -- to make something new.
We have destroyed each other with our politics of violent ideas and our wars of violent means...
And the only words of the Message I can still hear are:
"Begin again."
And it's my hope that we shall.
Over the last three years, the Endless Nation -- through war or other aggressive means -- now controls the former territories of the Republic and the Union.
In pulling them down, the Nation eradicated the systems of government that once ruled there and the vacuum left behind demands governance...
So -- right or wrong -- the Nation must continue to provide for them...as it is our burden. And in a right spirit, I now commit all three to peace...
If the elders see it in them not to object.

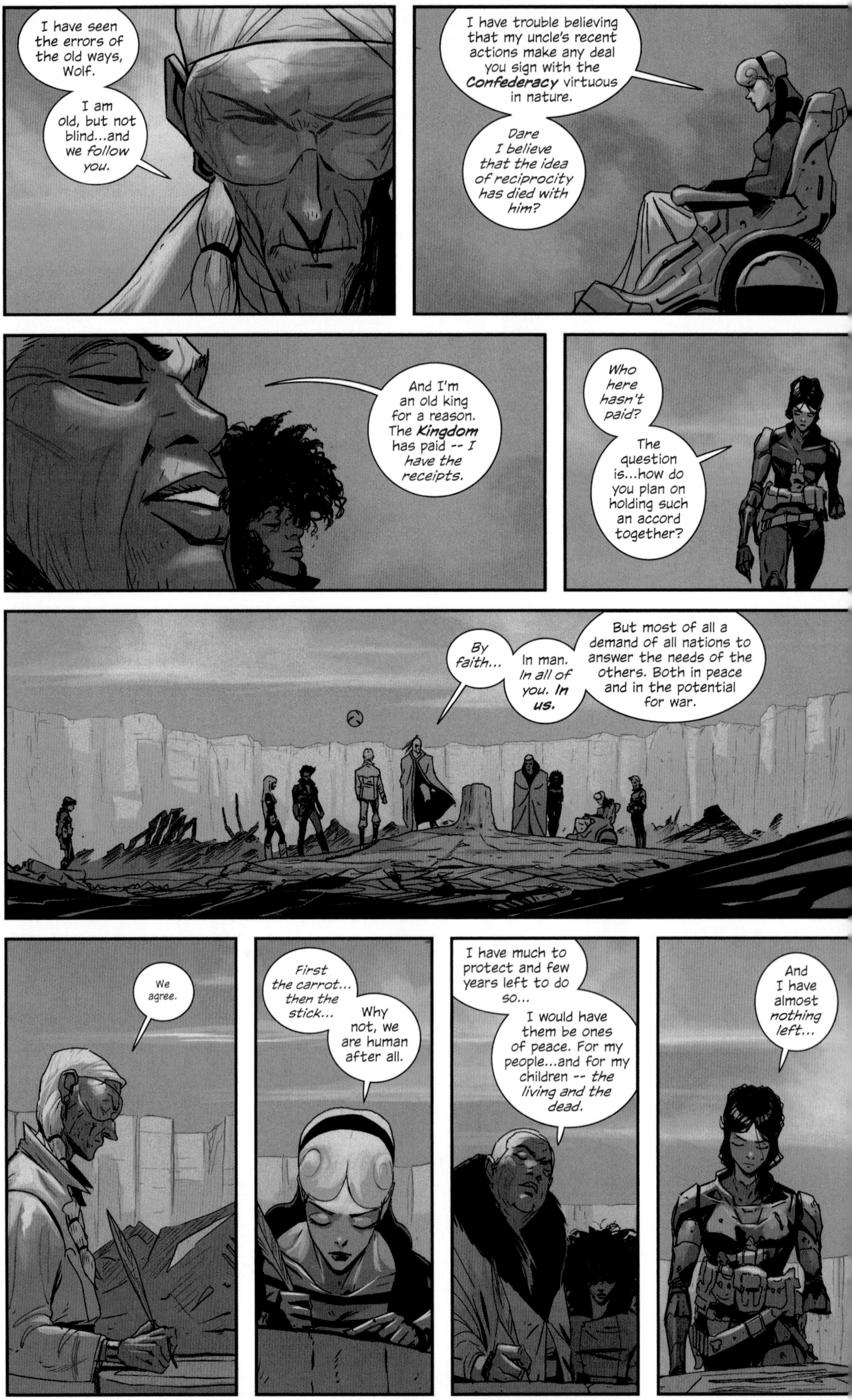

I have seen the errors of the old ways, Wolf.
I am old, but not blind...and we *follow* you.
I have trouble believing that my uncle's recent actions make any deal you sign with the **Confederacy** virtuous in nature.
Dare I believe that the idea of reciprocity has died with him?
And I'm an old king for a reason. The ***Kingdom*** has paid -- *I have the receipts.*
Who here hasn't paid?
The question is...how do you plan on holding such an accord together?
By faith...
In man. *In all of you.* ***In us.***
But most of all a demand of all nations to answer the needs of the others. Both in peace and in the potential for war.
We agree.
First the carrot... then the stick...
Why not, we are human after all.
I have much to protect and few years left to do so...
I would have them be ones of peace. For my people...and for my children -- *the living and the dead.*
And I have almost *nothing left...*

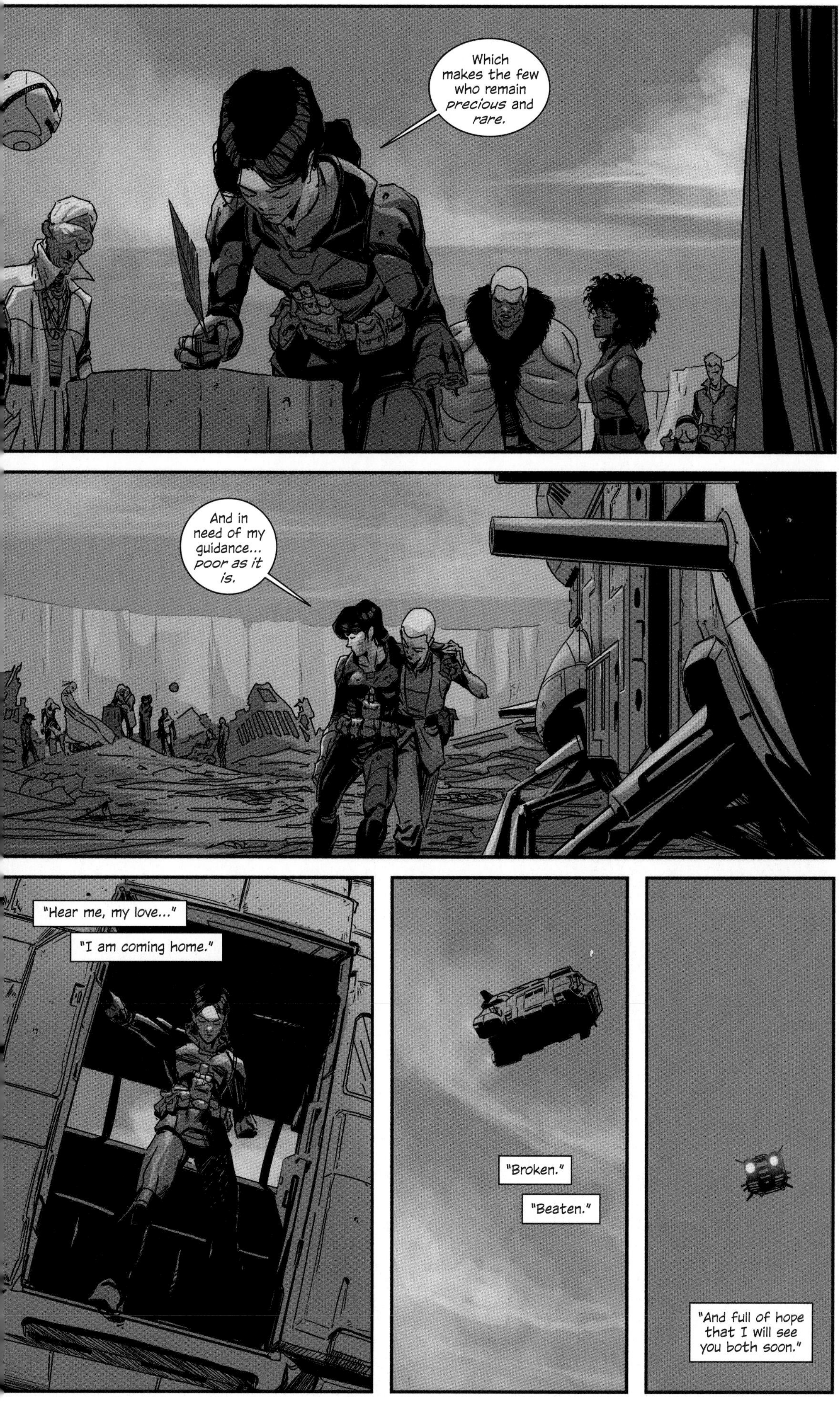
Which makes the few who remain *precious* and *rare.*
And in need of my guidance... *poor as it is.*
"Hear me, my love..."
"I am coming home."
"Broken."
"Beaten."
"And full of hope that I will see you both soon."

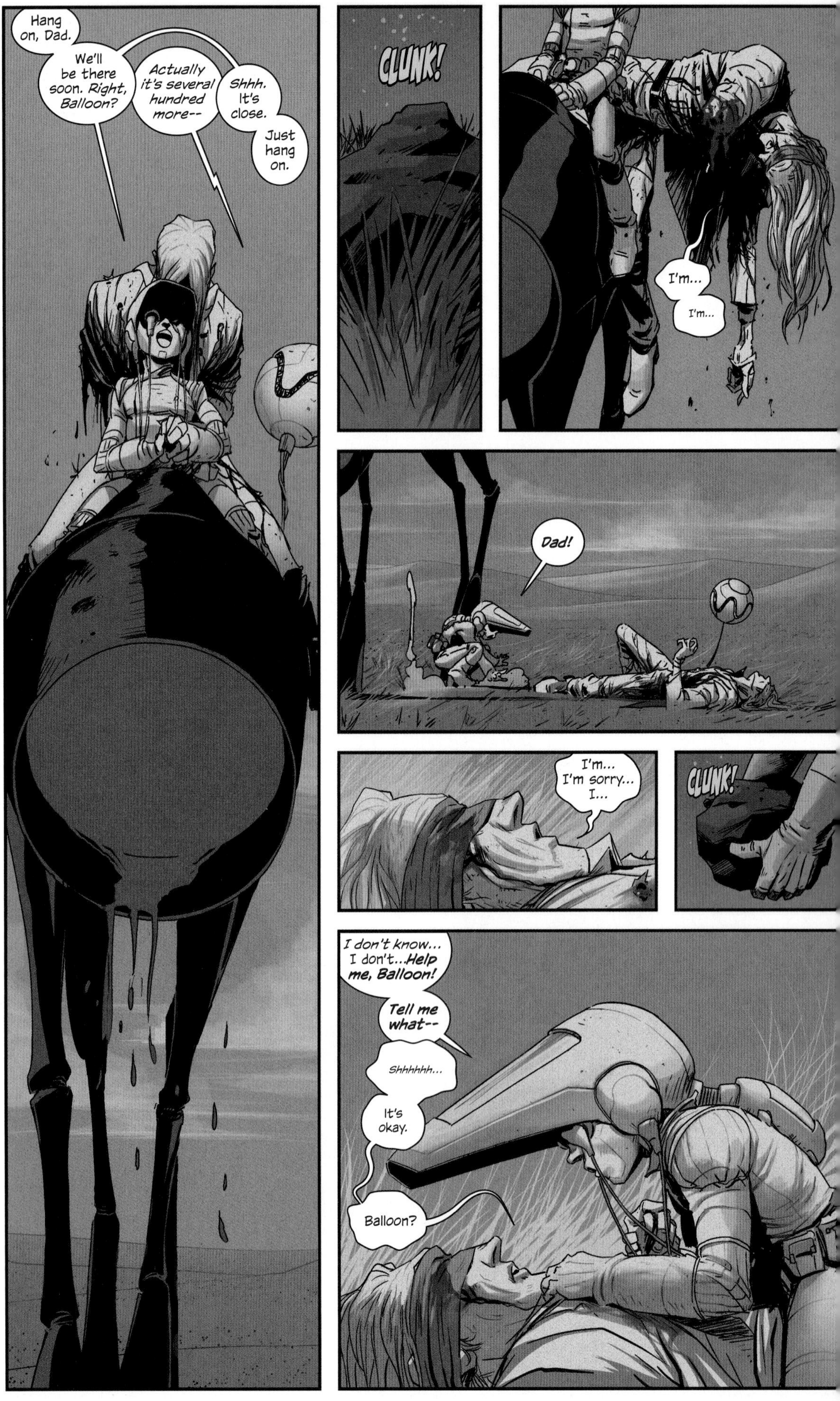
Hang on, Dad.
We'll be there soon. *Right,* Balloon?
Actually it's several hundred more--
Shhh. It's close.
Just hang on.
CLUNK!
I'm...
I'm...
Dad!
I'm... I'm sorry... I...
CLUNK!
*I don't know... I don't...***Help me, Balloon!**
Tell me what--
Shhhhhhh...
It's okay.
Balloon?

Yes?

You... you know what you have to do now, right?

Yes. I know. You can depend on me. We will find Xiaolian.

That's not what I mean. *And you know it.*

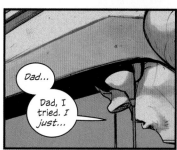

Dad...

Dad, I tried. I just...

I couldn't stop them. I'm...I'm sorry I couldn't *save* you.

Oh, son... *you did.*

A long time ago.

...

..

.

÷Sob!÷

÷Sniff.÷

CLUNK!
CLUNK!

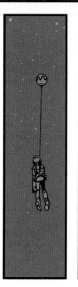

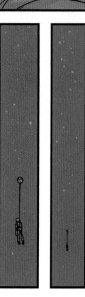

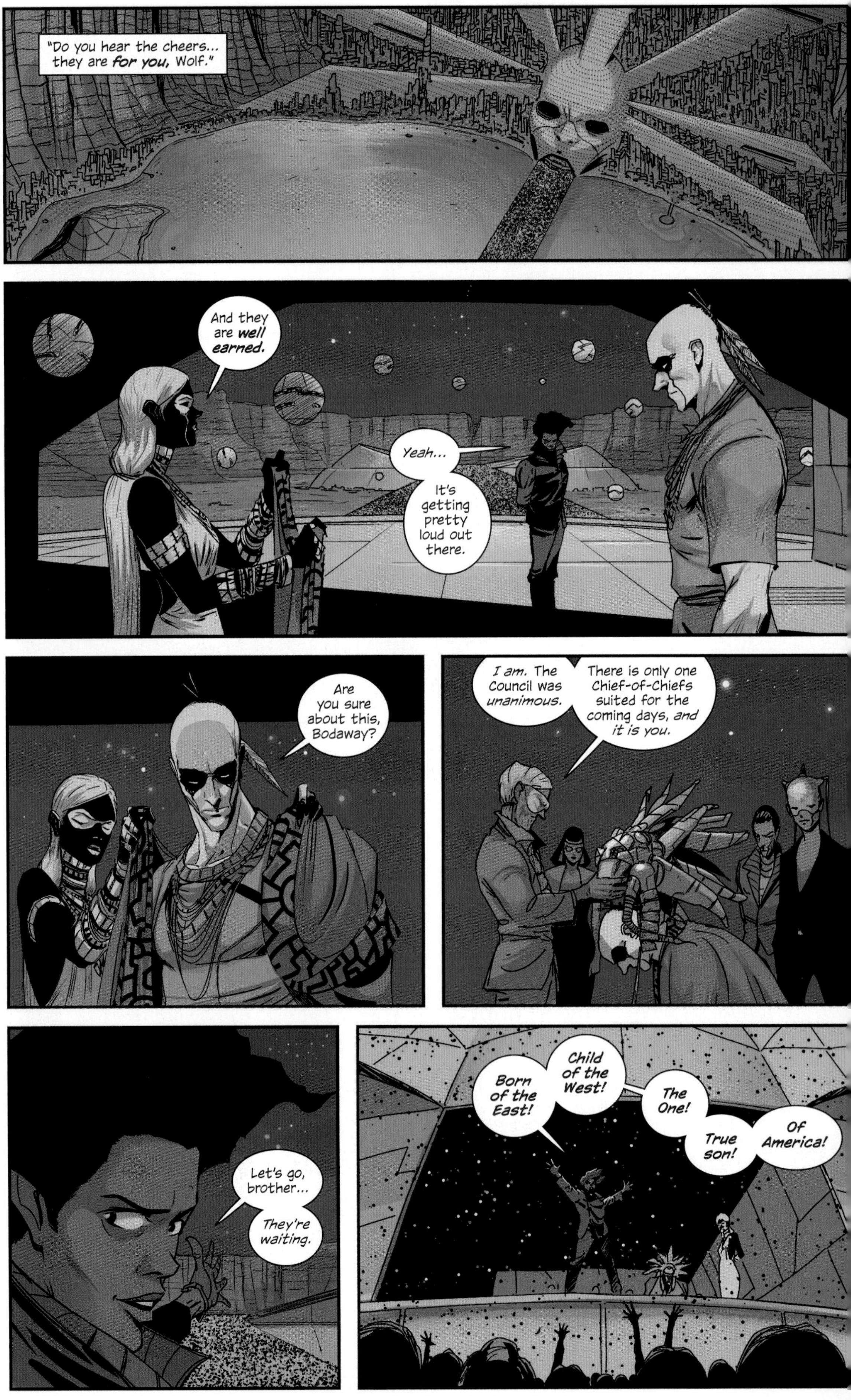
"Do you hear the cheers... they are *for you,* Wolf."
And they are ***well earned.***
Yeah...
It's getting pretty loud out there.
Are you sure about this, Bodaway?
I am. The Council was *unanimous.*
There is only one Chief-of-Chiefs suited for the coming days, *and it is you.*
Let's go, brother...
They're waiting.
Born of the East!
Child of the West!
The One!
True son!
Of America!

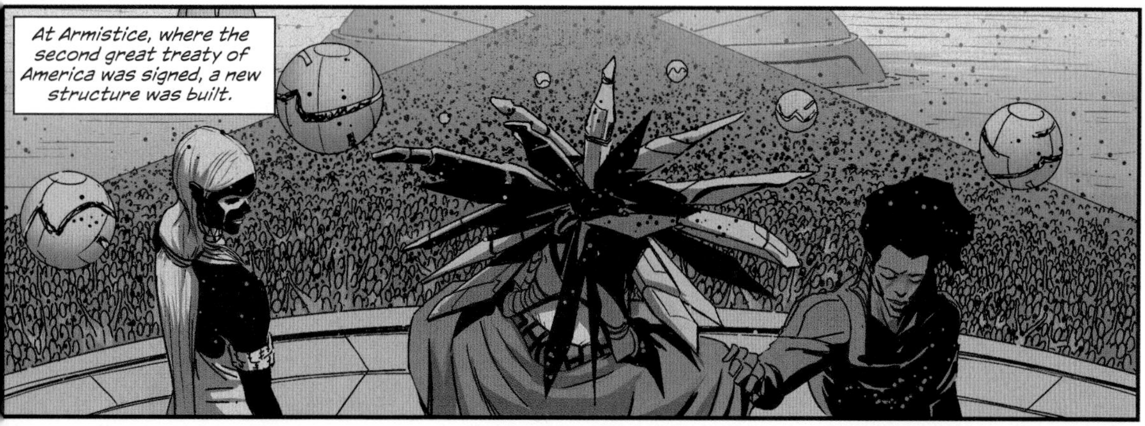
At Armistice, where the second great treaty of America was signed, a new structure was built.

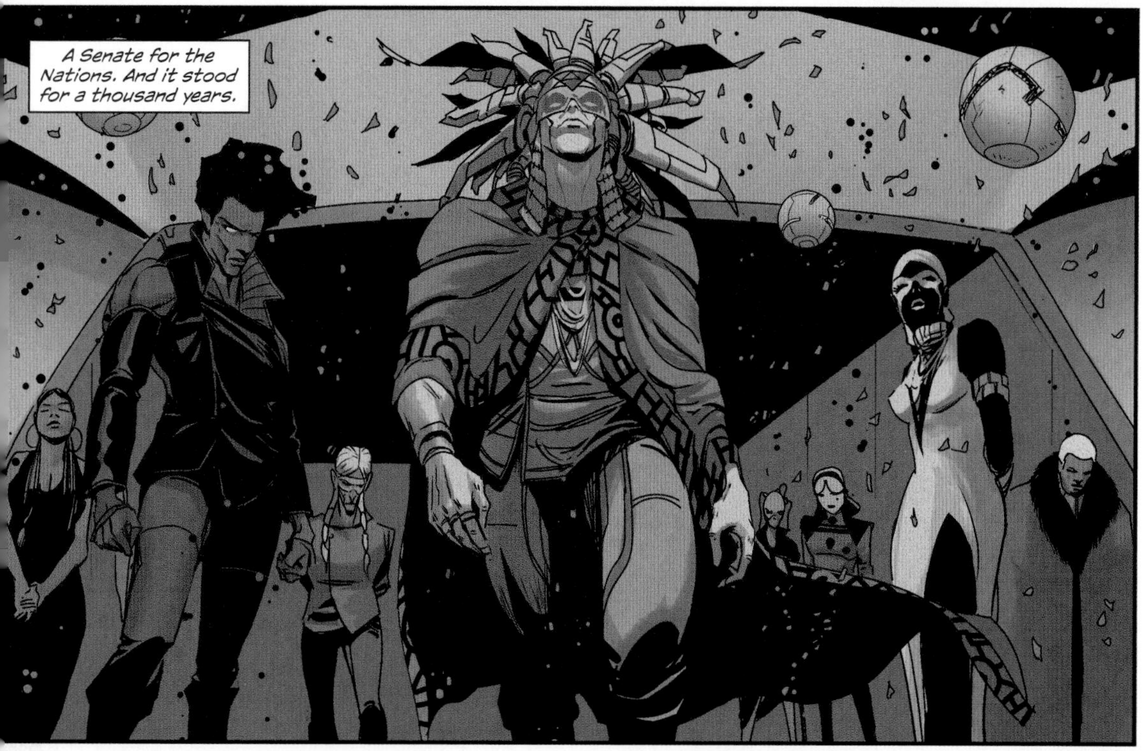
A Senate for the Nations. And it stood for a thousand years.

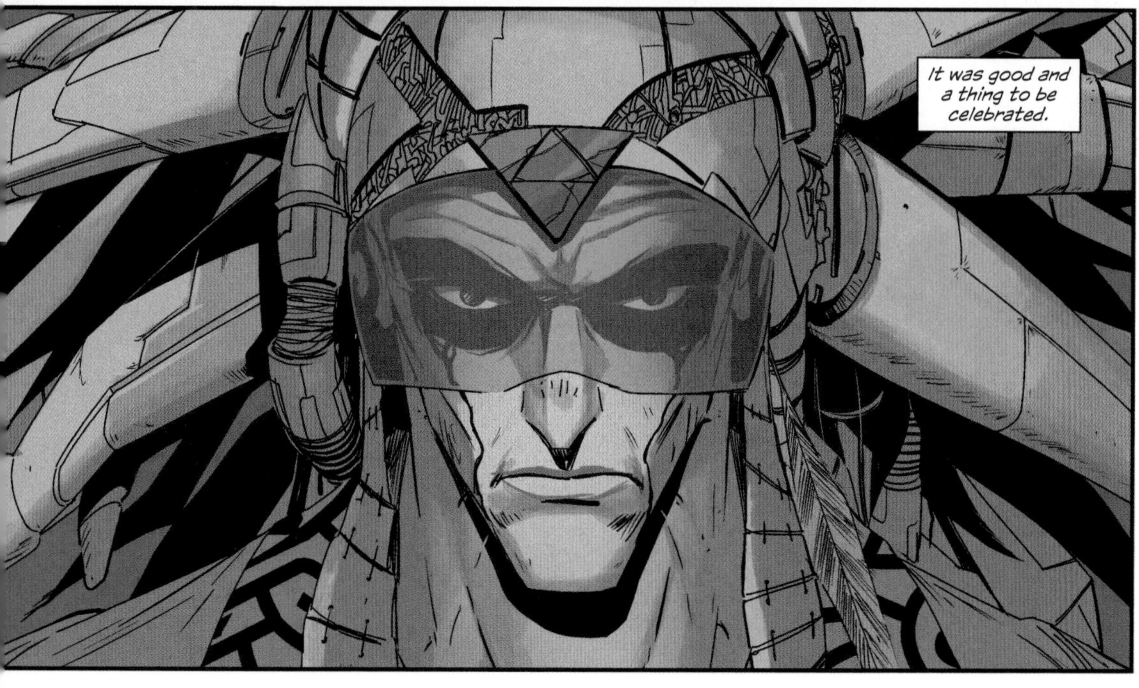
It was good and a thing to be celebrated.

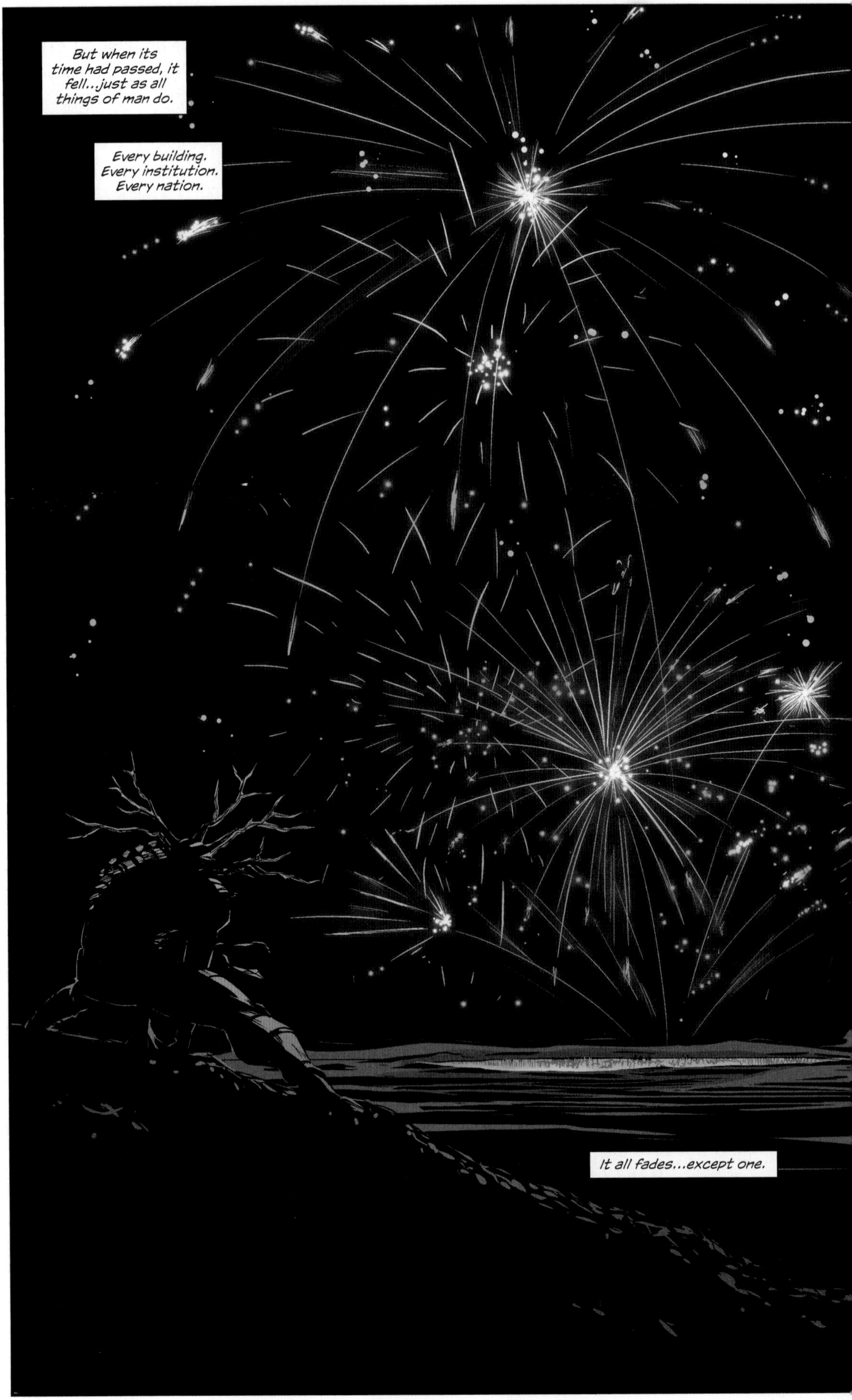
But when its time had passed, it fell...just as all things of man do.
Every building. Every institution. Every nation.
It all fades...except one.

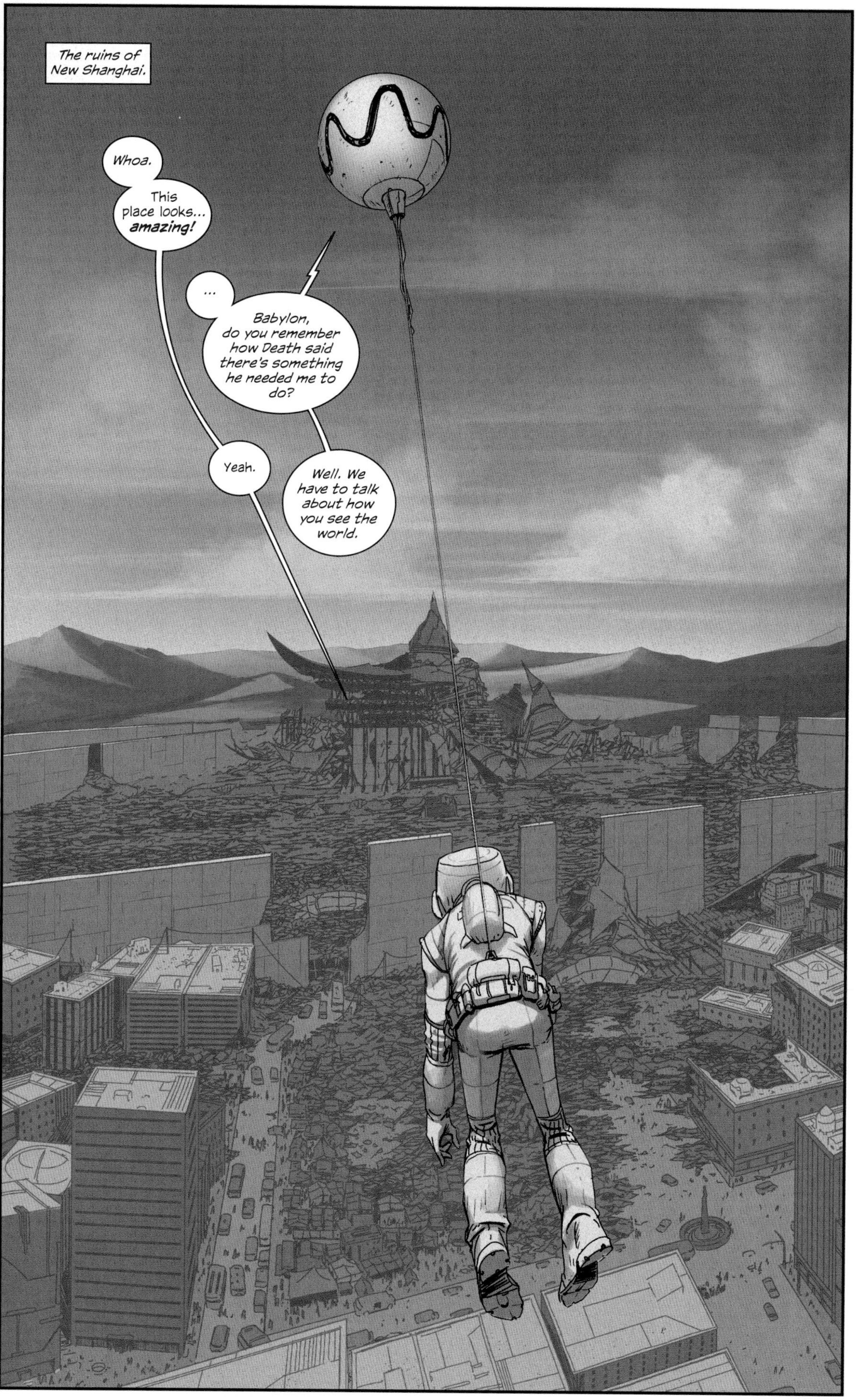

The ruins of New Shanghai.
Whoa.
This place looks... **amazing!**
...
Babylon, do you remember how Death said there's something he needed me to do?
Yeah.
Well. We have to talk about how you see the world.

Uh, infrared. Nightvision. Thermal.

I see just fine.

Always have.

Actually, you don't. That helmet you wear -- the one that connects you and me...it's... it's...

I know what it is. You run simulations.

You teach me what I'm *really seeing* when I look at the world.

It's how I've learned everything I know. *You taught me.*

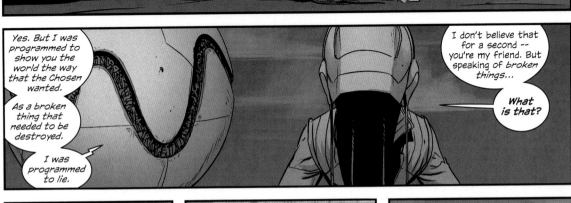

Yes. But I was programmed to show you the world the way that the Chosen wanted.

As a broken thing that needed to be destroyed.

I was programmed to lie.

I don't believe that for a second -- you're my friend. But speaking of *broken things*...

What is that?

Babylon?

Babylon?

Right, so about **that.**

Like I said, I was programmed to show you the world a certain way...

I didn't have a choice -- I had to...

As long as you're wearing that helmet.

Babylon?

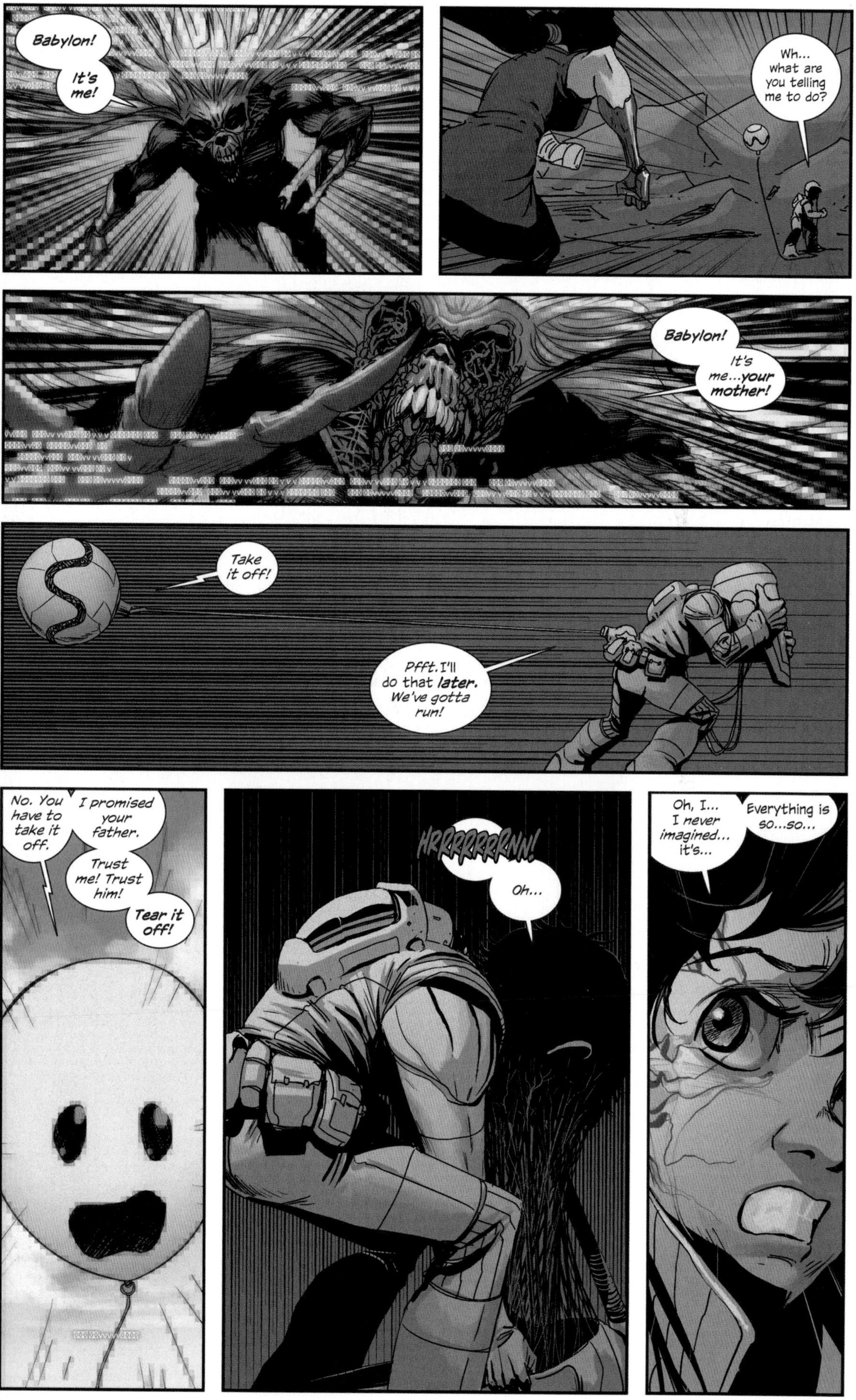

Babylon!
It's me!
Wh... what are you telling me to do?
Babylon!
It's me...your mother!
Take it off!
Pfft. I'll do that later. We've gotta run!
No. You have to take it off.
I promised your father.
Trust me! Trust him!
Tear it off!
HRRRRRRRNN!
Oh...
Oh, I... I never imagined... it's...
Everything is so...so...

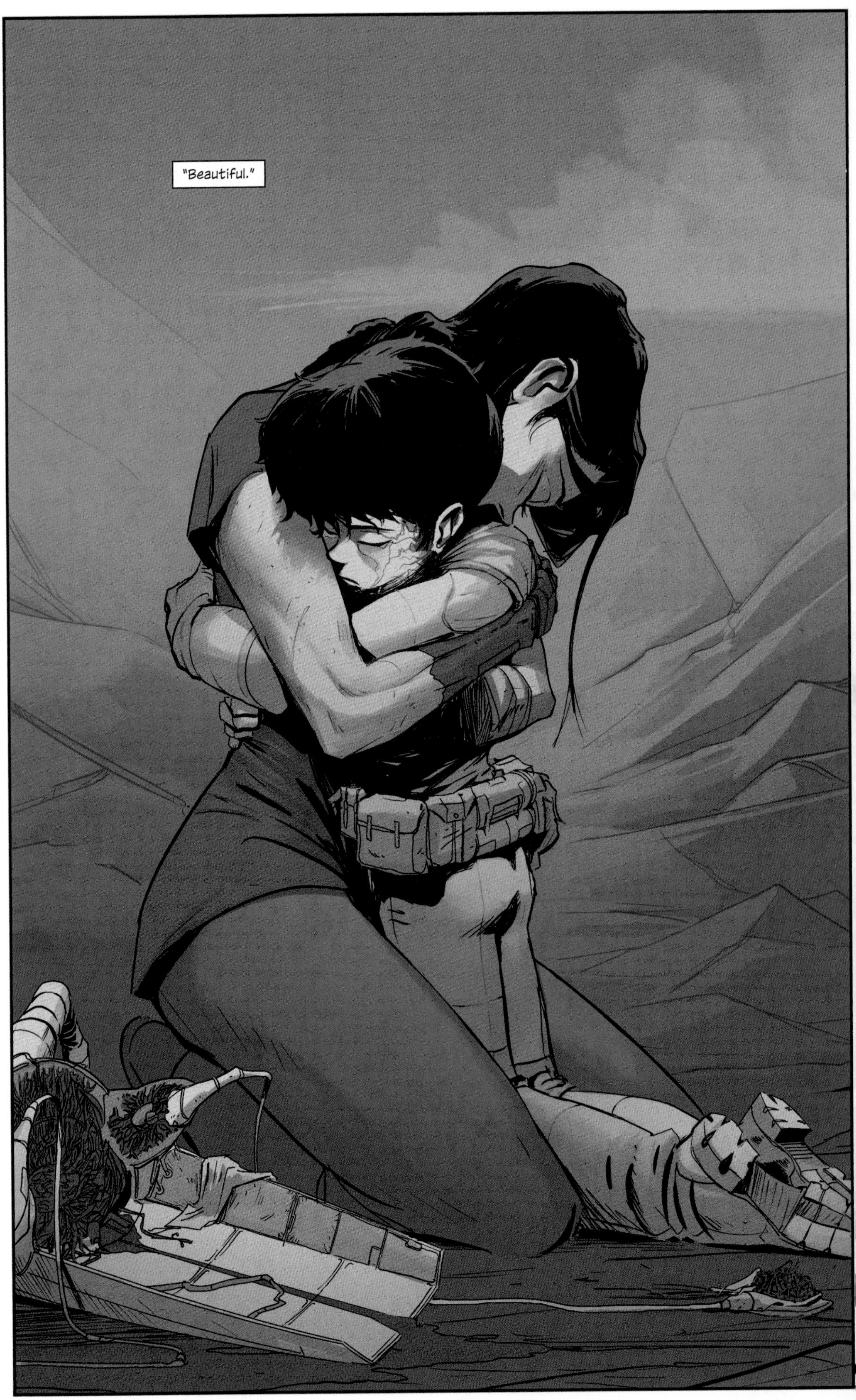
"Beautiful."

This is called progress, son...

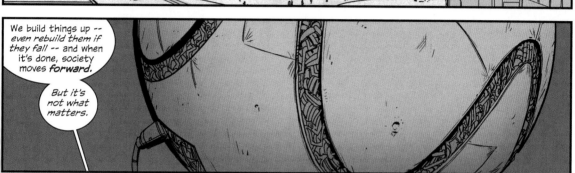

We build things up -- even rebuild them if they fall -- and when it's done, society moves *forward.*

But it's not what matters.

She's going to quote Death again, Babylon.

And there's a 92% chance that it's a saying you've already heard.

Yeah. Probably higher.

But I still want to hear her say it.

Here's what your father would've said:

It's easy to destroy things. To break them. To even *kill* them.

Nations. Buildings. People...

Everything in the world is just... *fragile.*

But what holds it *together* ain't at all.

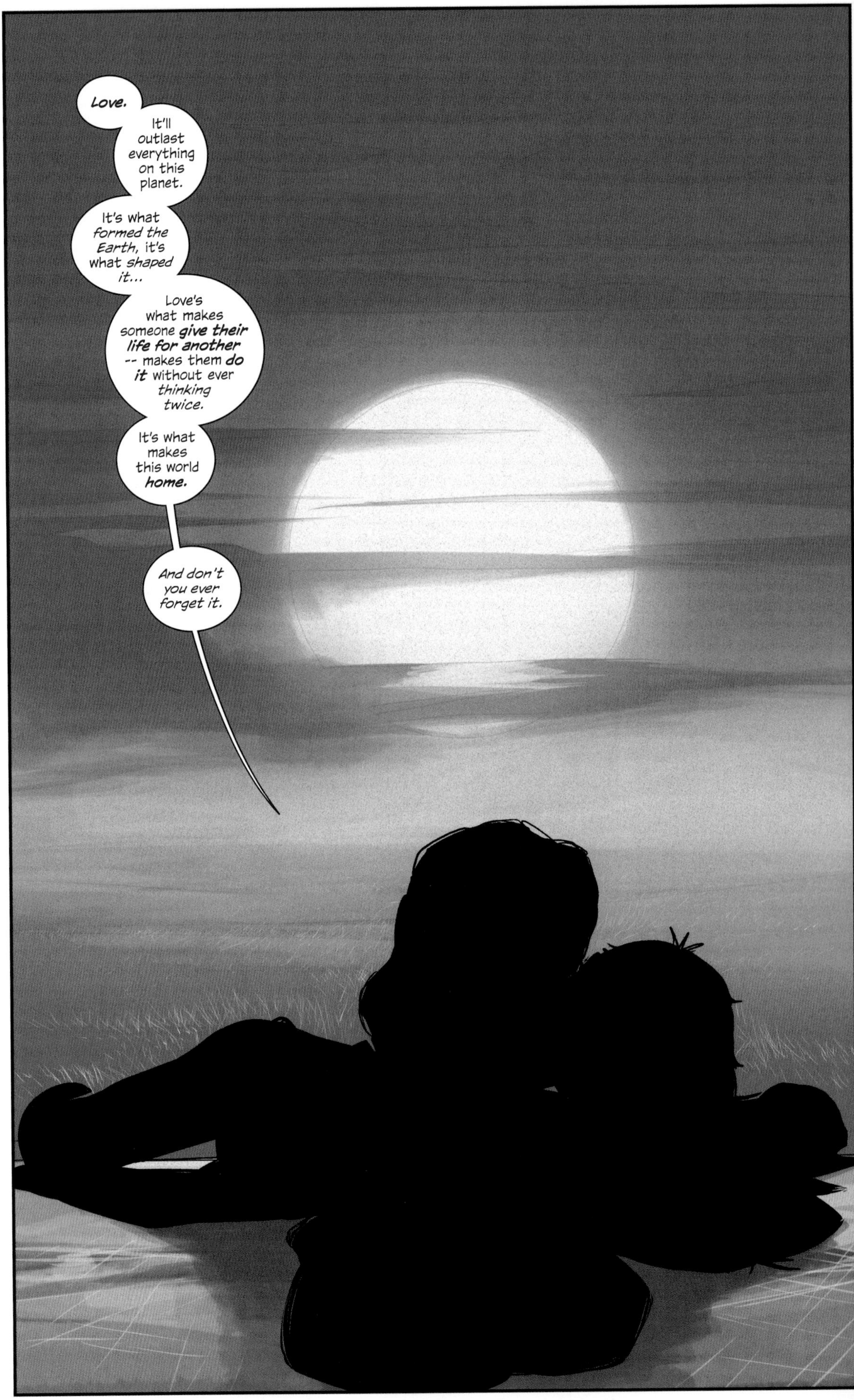
Love.
It'll outlast everything on this planet.
It's what formed the Earth, it's what shaped it...
Love's what makes someone give their life for another -- makes them do it without ever thinking twice.
It's what makes this world home.
And don't you ever forget it.

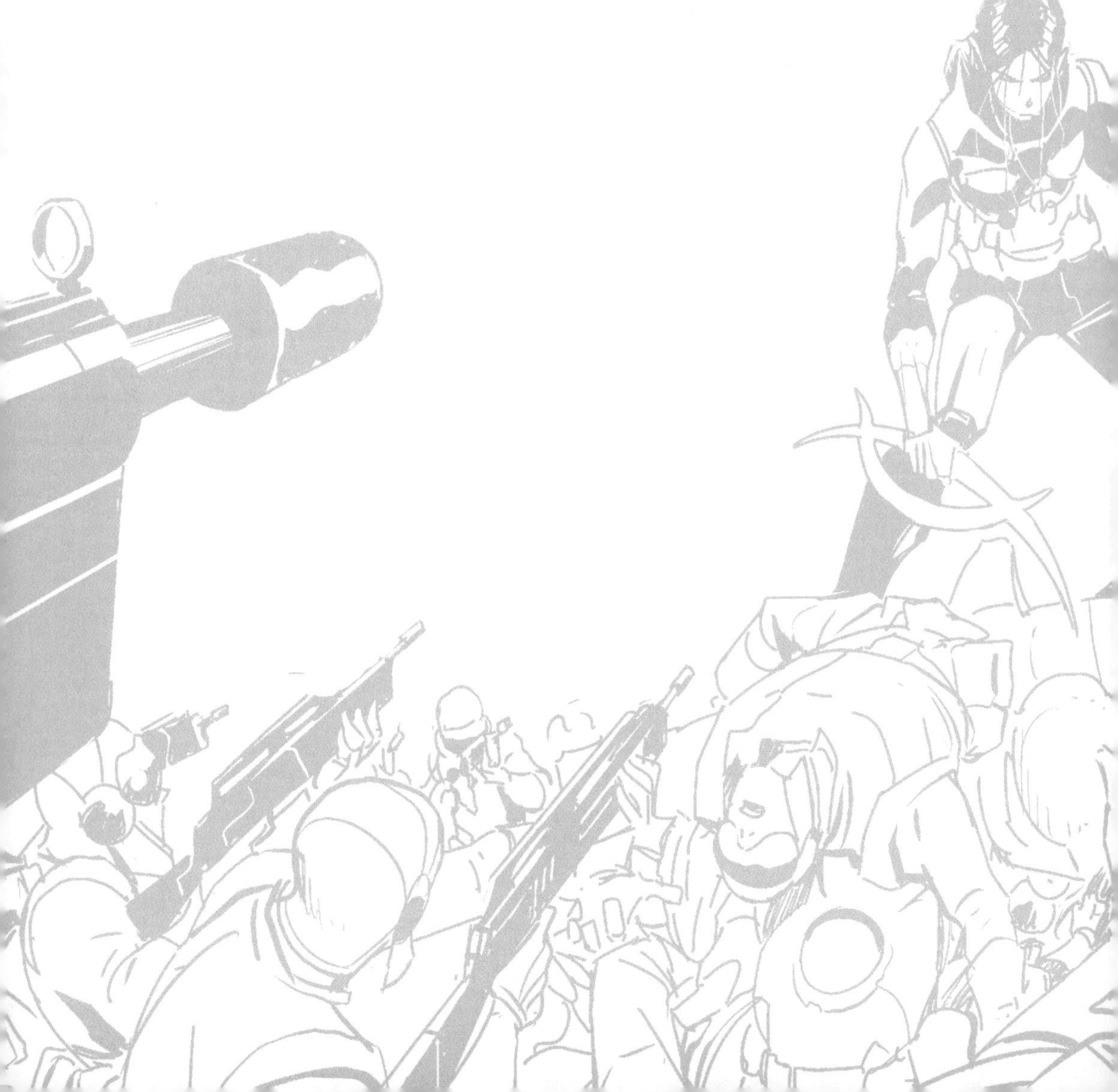

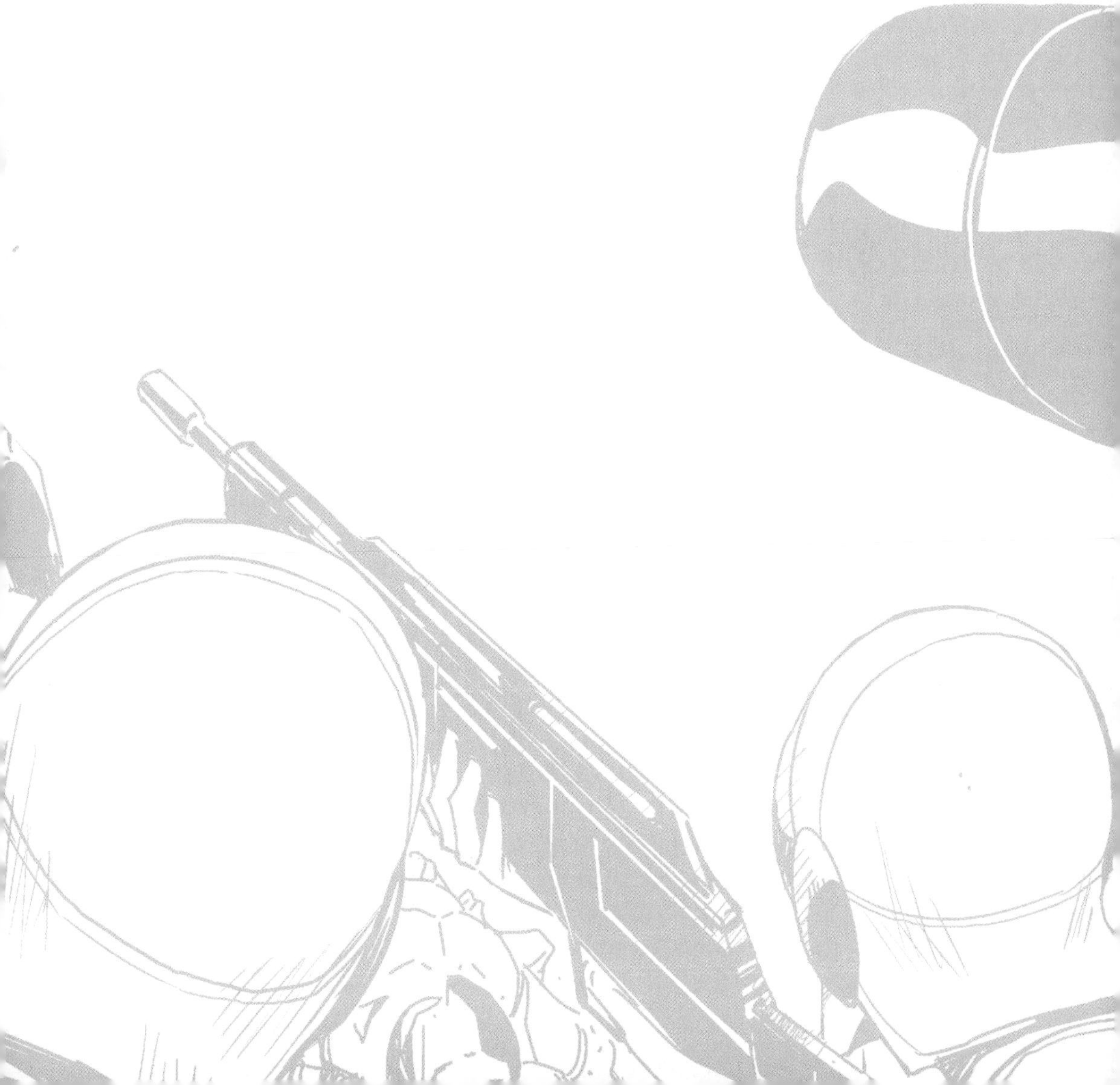

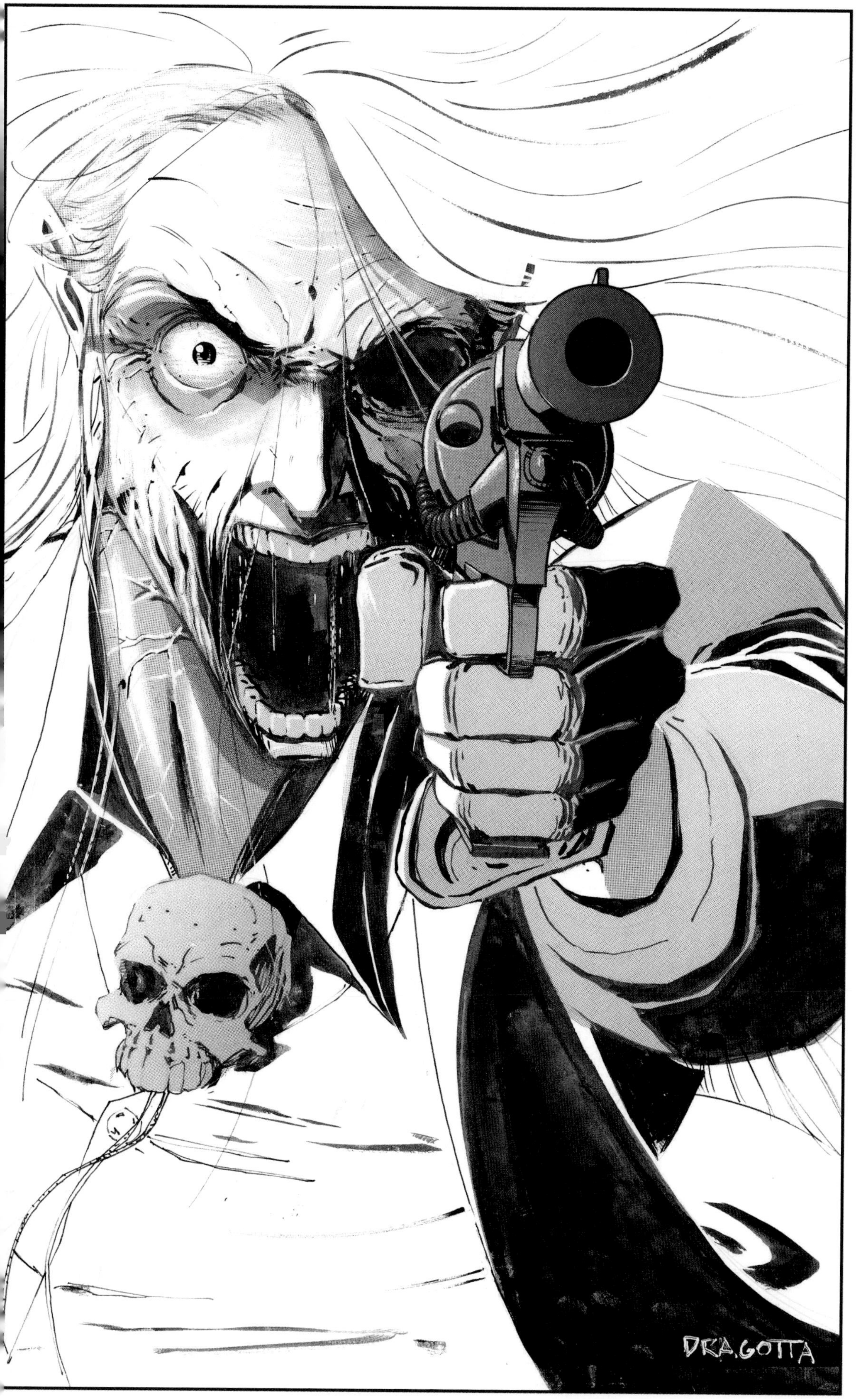
DRA.GOTTA

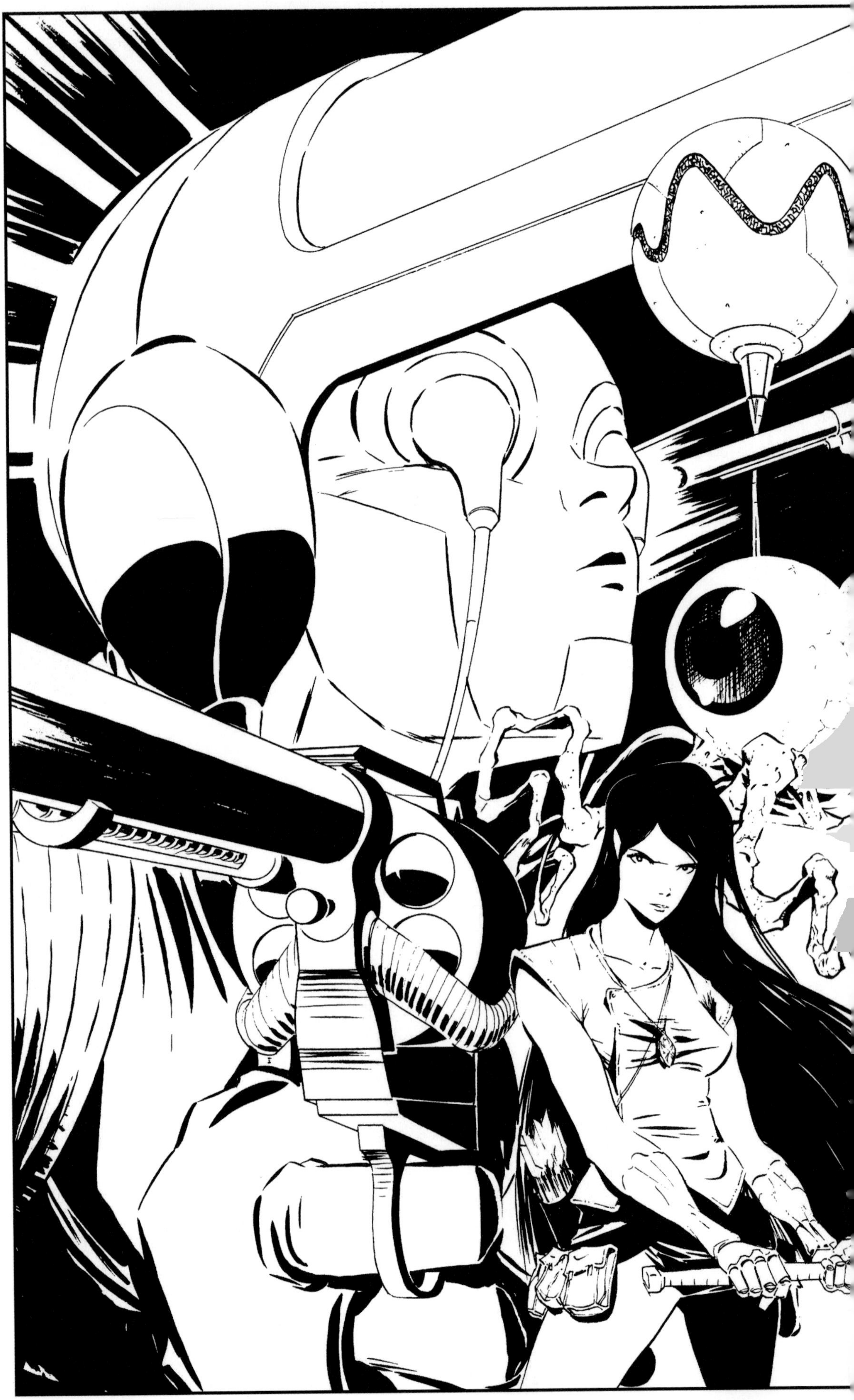

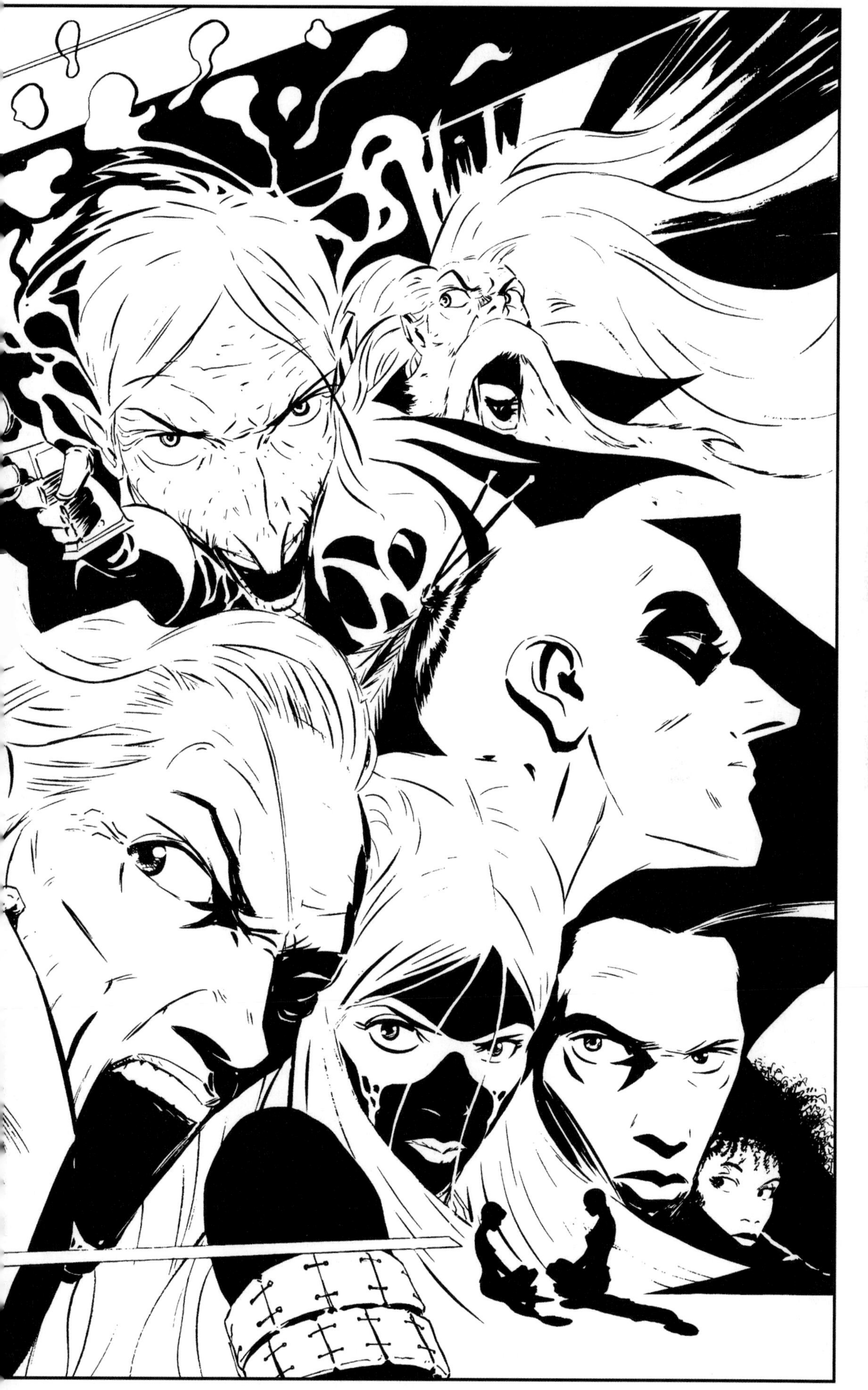

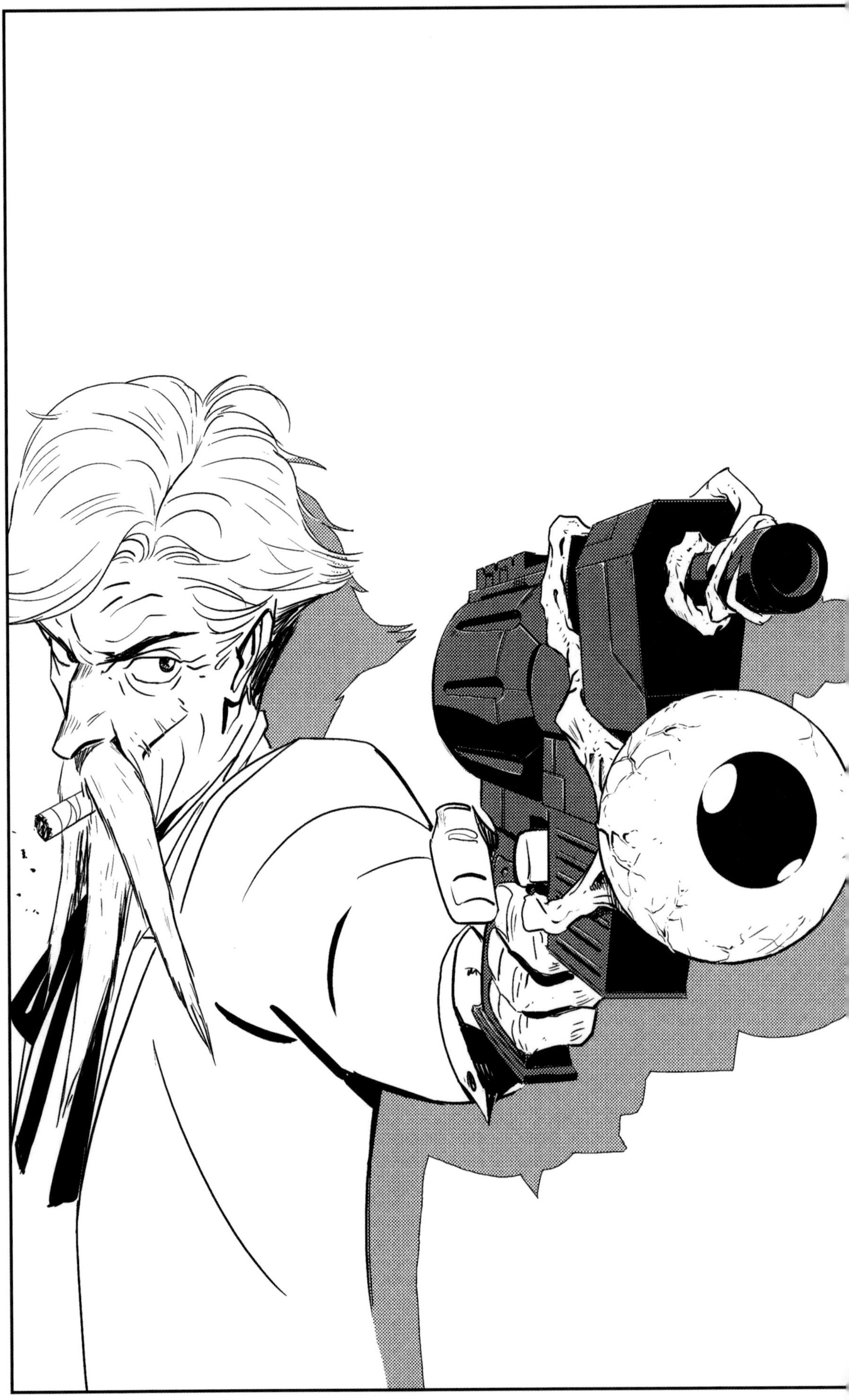

ALL MEN TELL **LIES.**
THESE ARE A **FEW** OF
THEM.

Jonathan Hickman is the visionary talent behind such works as the Eisner-nominated **NIGHTLY NEWS**, **THE MANHATTAN PROJECTS** and **PAX ROMANA**. He also plies his trade at MARVEL working on books like **FANTASTIC FOUR** and **THE AVENGERS**.

His twin brother, Marc, was just named the PGA caddie of the year.

Jonathan lives in South Carolina except when he doesn't.

You can visit his website: ***www.pronea.com***, or email him at: ***jonathan@pronea.com***.

.

Nick Dragotta's career began at Marvel Comics working on titles as varied as **X-STATIX, THE AGE OF THE SENTRY, X-MEN: FIRST CLASS, CAPTAIN AMERICA: FOREVER ALLIES** and **VENGEANCE**.

In addition, Nick is the co-creator of **HOWTOONS,** a comic series teaching kids how to build things and explore the world around them. **EAST OF WEST** is Nick's first creator-owned project at Image.